P9-BIC-750

granny square *Love*

A New *Twist* on a Crochet Classic for Your Home

sarah **london**

NORTH LIGHT BOOKS

CINCINNATI, OHIO

contents

introduction

Crochet, and granny squares in particular, have experienced a resurgence in popularity lately. They've been taking center stage worldwide, appearing on catwalks internationally, on telephone poles (as crochet graffiti) and in more and more homes. It seems the world has fallen in love with granny squares! And why wouldn't they?

My love of granny squares began at quite an early point in my life. As a child, I would sit and watch my grandmother crochet, creating individual granny squares, each bursting with color. In turn, she would join the squares to form multicolored blankets of warmth and love. It was the colors that really captured my attention. Squares alive with wicked bold color combinations sang to my heart.

The essence of this book is to introduce crochet (and color) to your home with granny squares as your starting point. If you have "Learn to crochet" on your to-do list, I hope this book will inspire you to pick up a hook and begin. If you are an experienced crocheter wishing to ignite your work with a little more color, but you're at a loss about where to begin, let the color discussion accompanying each project encourage you to go forth boldly to experiment with color. Dare to incorporate unexpected color combinations—you'll be surprised at the wonderful results.

After learning the tips, tricks and techniques of crochet in the first chapter, you'll find projects for each room of your home in the following chapters. If you've never crocheted before, begin with a cushion. An injection of bright, bold color in the form of crocheted cushions will transform your living room in an instant. Or a cozy crocheted blanket is always welcomed when the weather turns cold. Try one in a mix of colors; either of the blankets featured in this book would provide color and comfort throughout the winter. For an unconventional twist on granny squares, you'll find plenty of inspiration in these pages. For example, the Grocer's Tote on page 66 is perfect for fashionably running to the grocery store or farmer's market. Crochet-covered hangers like the ones on page 122 make superb gifts and can be made quickly; they're great for last-minute gifts. Or try plunging your toes into a cozy crocheted mat like the one on page 130 as you step out of the shower! I hope throughout the pages you will find projects that appeal to you and color combinations that stop you in your tracks and inspire you to dress your home with color.

Today's the day—pick up a hook and a skein of yarn, and color your world with granny squares!

chapter one

Getting Started

Granny squares, to me, are the foundation of crochet. By embarking on your crochet journey with basic granny squares, you will gain the confidence to progress to more intricate patterns as well as fancier stitches and textures in no time.

In this chapter you'll find everything you need to be off to a good beginning. The beauty of crochet is that you only need a skein of yarn and a crochet hook to begin, and we'll cover both of those here. Plus, granny squares involve only a few relatively simple stitches. Study the stitch diagrams; once you've mastered the basic stitches, the sky's the limit. Hook a few practice swatches of each stitch, and then try your hand at projects in the following chapters.

Relax and crochet with confidence, and soon you'll be hooked!

materials

The tools and materials for crochet are quite simple: for every project, start by picking a crochet hook and yarn.

Crochet hooks come in many different sizes, colors and materials. They can be made of aluminum, plastic, wood and even bamboo. Personally, I'm drawn to brightly colored anodized aluminum crochet hooks. The two most important factors to consider when choosing a hook are picking the right size for your project and selecting a hook that is comfortable in your hand and easy for you to use. A list of crochet hook sizes can be found in General Crochet Information on page 138.

After a crochet hook comes yarn. Yarn, glorious yarn, comes in many different colors, textures, weights and compositions. Admittedly, I'm taken by color and place less emphasis on composition. I like to mix things up a bit and sometimes combine both pure wool and acrylic into one project. You can do the same, or follow your own preferences. All of the projects in this book were hooked with Cascade 220, a 100 percent pure wool yarn. Cascade 220 boasts an enormous color palette and is absolutely divine to work with.

When you choose a yarn, consider the end use of your project, and refer to the care instructions on the band that accompanies each skein of yarn so you know how to take care of the finished project. If it's going to receive a lot of wear and tear, consider using a machine-washable yarn. If you have crocheted a scrumptious blanket and intend to gift it to someone special, include a band from the yarn used so the recipient will know how to care for the item correctly.

Next, you need to consider how the hook and yarn will interact. On the band of each skein of yarn you'll notice a suggested hook size that is recommended when working with that particular yarn. Remember that this is only a suggestion: If you find your work is too loose, go down a hook size; alternatively, if you find that your work is too tight, go up a hook size. Sample different yarns and hooks until you find a combination that creates a fabric you like. You can find more about yarn and gauge in General Crochet Information as well.

Ultimately, both hook and yarn choices will be influenced by personal preference and budget. Experiment with different yarns until you find a favorite, and likewise with crochet hooks. Set aside a little "pin money" for when it comes time for your next yarn splurge.

After you have chosen your hook and yarn, you'll only need to add a yarn needle (for sewing in ends) and scissors (for trimming yarn tails). If you like, you can also use some of the numerous crochet accessories on the market to make your crochet experience easier and more enjoyable.

Keeping Track

When I start a new project, I keep the ball bands from the yarns used and staple a sample of the yarn to the band. This gives me a quick visual record of the yarns from the project that I can go back to again and again.

basic crochet stitches

Over the next few pages you'll find step-by-step instructions for basic crochet stitches and granny squares. As you follow these instructions, the most important thing to remember is to relax. Take a deep breath and sit comfortably as you practice. When teaching crochet classes in the past, I've noticed that if you are rigid and tense when you crochet, it will show in your work. Your tension will be tight, which in turn makes it difficult to maneuver your crochet hook into the stitches. I have also witnessed people holding their breath, maybe from concentrating too hard to perfect each wrap of the yarn. Please remember to exhale! Breathe and relax with each stitch performed. Crochet is soothing for the soul after all.

Start by tensioning the yarn with your hand. You can thread the yarn under and over your fingers, or you can wrap the yarn around your little finger to tension it. Use any method that allows you to control the flow of the yarn through your hand. Hold the hook however you feel most comfortable. Some prefer to hold the hook like a pencil; others prefer a grip like they'd use on a bicycle handlebar. There is no right or wrong way—do what works for you, and make sure not to grip the crochet hook too tightly.

slip knot

Use this easy knot at the beginning of every project to attach the yarn to the crochet hook.

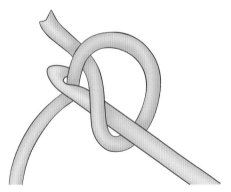

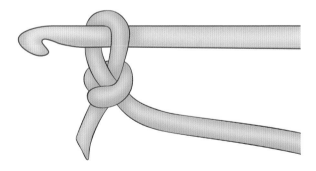

1 Create a loop near the end of the yarn. Insert the hook into the loop, and catch the strand of yarn connected to the skein.

2 Pull the yarn through the loop. Gently tug on the yarn to tighten the loop around the hook.

chain stitch (ch)

Chain stitches are often used at the start of a project and can also be used to travel from area to area within a project.

1 Wrap the yarn around the hook, and draw it through the loop on the hook. One chain made.

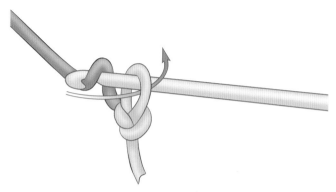

single crochet (sc)

A single crochet is a short, compact stitch.

1 Insert the hook into a stitch, wrap the yarn around the hook, and draw the yarn through only the first loop on the hook.

2 Wrap the yarn around the hook again, and draw the yarn through both loops on the hook. One single crochet made.

half double crochet (hdc)

This stitch is taller than the single crochet stitch because it includes an additional wrap.

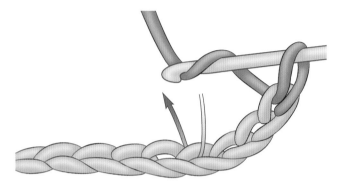

1 Wrap the yarn around the hook, and then insert the hook into a stitch.

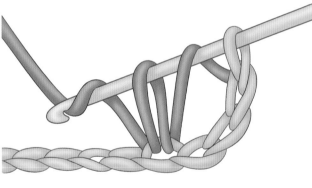

2 Wrap the yarn around the hook, and draw the yarn through the first loop on the hook. Wrap the yarn around the hook again.

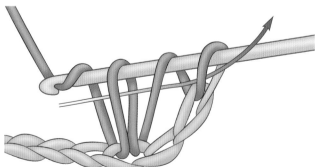

3 Draw the yarn through all 3 loops on the hook. One half double crochet made.

double crochet (dc)

An additional step taken during this stitch makes it taller than single and half double crochet stitches. This stitch is very common in granny squares.

1 Follow Steps 1–2 of Half Double Crochet on page 14. Draw the yarn through the first 2 loops on the hook. Wrap the yarn around the hook a last time, and draw the yarn through the remaining 2 loops on the hook. One double crochet made.

slip stitch (sl st)

This stitch is used to move the hook and yarn to a new place in the crochet and adds almost no height.

1 Insert the hook into the next stitch, wrap the yarn around the hook, and draw the yarn through both loops on the hook. One slip stitch made.

making granny squares

The basic structure of a granny square is groups of double crochet stitches separated by chain stitches. On each subsequent row, the groups of double crochet stitches are made into the chain spaces in the previous row. Corners are formed by placing two groups of double crochet stitches in the corner chain spaces. I've broken down the general process here for you to practice; for each project, follow the instructions for the granny squares in that pattern.

1 Begin with a slip knot. Chain 5. Make a slip stitch in the first stitch of the chain to form a ring. Chain 3.

2 Work 2 double crochet into the ring. The chain plus 2 stitches makes up the first group of double crochet stitches. Chain 2.

3 Work 3 double crochet into the ring.

4 Chain 2, work 3 more double crochet into the ring. And then once more, chain 2, work 3 double crochet into the ring. Chain 2. The ring now has four groups of three double crochet worked into it.

5 Join with a slip stitch into the top of the beginning chain 3. The first round is complete.

6 Slip stitch across the next 2 stitches and into the corner space.

7 Cut the yarn and secure it. Join a new color in any corner space simply by tying a knot.

8 Chain 3. Work (2 double crochet, chain 2, 3 double crochet) into the corner space. Chain 1.

9 Work (3 double crochet, chain 2, 3 double crochet) into the next corner space. Chain 1.

10 Repeat Step 9 all the way around the square. Join with a slip stitch into the top of the beginning chain 3. Round 2 is complete.

11 Slip stitch across the next 2 stitches and into the corner space. Cut the yarn and secure it. Join a new color in any corner space simply by tying a knot. Chain 3. Work (2 double crochet, chain 2, 3 double crochet) into the corner space. Chain 1. Work 3 double crochet into the next chain-1 space, chain 1.

12 Work (3 double crochet, chain 2, 3 double crochet) into the corner space. Chain 1. Work 3 double crochet into the next chain-1 space, chain 1. Repeat around the square until Round 3 is complete. Repeat Steps 11–12 for each new round, working 1 group of 3 double crochet in each chain-space along the side and 2 groups of 3 double crochet into each corner.

reading patterns and charts

Each project in this book begins with a materials list that gives you vital information about the project: First, you'll find a list of the yarns and yarn colors used in the project. Next, the hook(s) and notions are listed. Finally, you'll find the finished measurements of the project. Each of these pieces of information is important, but they aren't set in stone—you can customize your projects to suit your needs. If you want to change the colors used, or even the number of colors used, feel free! If you don't like the way your project feels with the suggested hook size, try a different hook. To make a firmer fabric, use a smaller hook. To make a softer, drapier fabric, use a larger hook. If you want a larger project, add more rows or rounds, or add more blocks. For a smaller project, remove rows, rounds or blocks. Don't be afraid to tweak my instructions to make a project your own.

After the materials list, the project's pattern is provided in two formats: written and charted. The written instructions tell you what stitches are made in what order for each row or round of the pattern. Much of the written instructions contain abbreviations. A list of the abbreviations used in this book can be found on page 138.

The charted instruction is a visual representation of the pattern, with each stitch represented by a symbol. A chart showing the symbols used in this book can be found on page 138. When working a stitch diagram in the round, look to the center of the diagram, find the starting chain and start there. When working a stitch diagram in rows, look to the bottom of the diagram, find the starting chain and use that as your starting point. The numbers in bold on the diagrams indicate the row or round number. Alternating rows or rounds are shown in different colors to help distinguish between them. If you are new to using charts to crochet, I suggest you try using them here. Compare the written instructions to the charted instructions as you work so you can "translate" the charted pattern using the written instructions. On some of the larger patterns, the charted instructions are only shown in part; use the portion that is charted as a guideline for completing the portions that are not charted.

If you ever feel overwhelmed by the instructions, take a deep breath, and remember that crochet is worked just one stitch at a time. Focus on your next stitch, and when it's done, focus on the one after that. Before you know it, you'll have a beautiful finished project!

chapter two

The Living Room

In this chapter you will find six zippy projects to spruce up your living room in an instant! One or two colorful crocheted cushions will introduce color to your living room quickly. They'll smarten your sofa, as well as provide comfort. Or, take cushions to the next level with an extra-large cushion that will provide casual seating for impromptu gatherings. The larger-than-life cushion on page 28 is perfect for children and grown-ups alike to lounge on.

There is nothing more satisfying or gratifying than giving a worn or dated object a face-lift. Try the Lampshade Cover on page 32; with a small pile of crocheted granny squares, you will be able to make over a drum lampshade and create a statement piece for your living room that is truly unique. Don't stop dressing up your living room there either! Refresh an old (or new) ottoman with a slipcover; it will not only enhance your living room, but also allow extra color to filter into your surroundings. Of course, for me (and maybe for you too!), a living room would not be complete without a lively granny square blanket that sings with color. More is more when it comes to making granny square blankets—gather as many colors as possible to work a blanket that really pops.

The final project in this chapter isn't one you'll use every day, but you'll be happy to have it when a certain time of year rolls around. Oh, the anticipation on children's faces when they hang their Christmas stockings on the mantel come Christmas Eve! Worked in the traditional granny square stitch, use the pattern on page 44 to make a Christmas stocking for each member of your family. Your handiwork is sure to be treasured and loved for many future Christmases.

square cushion

Colorful crocheted cushions will transform and lift your living room in an instant! This striking geometric design will never look outdated or tired. Mix and match your color combinations for each cushion to coordinate with your décor. Or be bold and work cushions in clashing color combinations to add a little zing to your space.

yarn

4 skeins worsted weight yarn,
1 each of 4 colors (A, B, C and D)

The cushions shown here were made using Cascade 220 (100% Peruvian highland wool, 3.5oz/100g, 220yd/201m). Cushion 1 uses colors #8895 (A), #7804 (B), #9470 (C) and #8010 (D). Cushion 2 uses colors #7827 (A), #8408 (B), #7825 (C) and #8010 (D).

crochet hook

U.S. size G/6 (4mm)

notions

14" (35.5cm) square pillow form

5 buttons, ½" (13mm) diameter

Yarn needle

finished measurements

Approx. 14" (35.5cm) square

front

With color A, ch 5, join with a sl st to form a ring.

RND 1: Ch 3, work 2 dc into the ring, * ch 2, work 3 dc into the ring; rep from * twice more, ch 2, join with a sl st into top of beg ch-3. Sl st across the next 2 sts and into the corner sp.

RND 2: Ch 3, work (2 dc, ch 2, 3 dc) into corner sp, * ch 1, work (3 dc, ch 2, 3 dc) into next ch-2 corner sp; rep from * twice more, ch 1, join with a sl st into top of beg ch-3. Sl st across the next 2 sts and into the corner sp.

RND 3: Ch 3, work (2 dc, ch 2, 3 dc) into corner sp, * ch 1, work 3 dc into ch-1 sp, ch 1, work (3 dc, ch 2, 3 dc) into next ch-2 corner sp; rep from * twice more, ch 1, work 3 dc into ch-1 sp, ch 1, join with a sl st into top of beg ch-3. Sl st across the next 2 sts and into the corner sp.

RND 4: Ch 3, work (2 dc, ch 2, 3 dc) into corner sp, * ch 1, [work 3 dc into ch-1 sp, ch 1] twice, work (3 dc, ch 2, 3 dc) into next ch-2 corner sp; rep from * twice more, ch 1, [work 3 dc into ch-1 sp, ch 1] twice, join with a sl st into top of beg ch-3. Sl st across the next 2 sts and into the corner sp. Fasten off A.

RND 5: Join color B into any ch-2 corner sp, ch 3, work (2 dc, ch 2, 3 dc) into corner sp, * ch 1, [work 3 dc into ch-1 sp, ch 1] 3 times, work (3 dc, ch 2, 3 dc) into next ch-2 corner sp; rep from * twice more, ch 1, [work 3 dc into ch-1 sp, ch 1] 3 times, join with a sl st into top of beg ch-3. Sl st across the next 2 sts and into the corner sp.

RND 6: Ch 3, work (2 dc, ch 2, 3 dc) into corner sp, * ch 1, [work 3 dc into ch-1 sp, ch 1] 4 times, work (3 dc, ch 2, 3 dc) into next ch-2 corner sp; rep from * twice more, ch 1, [work 3 dc into ch-1 sp, ch 1] 4 times, join with a sl st into top of beg ch-3. Sl st across the next 2 sts and into the corner sp. Fasten off B.

RND 7: Join color C into any ch-2 corner sp, ch 3, work (2 dc, ch 2, 3 dc) into corner sp, * ch 1, [work 3 dc into ch-1 sp, ch 1] 5 times, work (3 dc, ch 2, 3 dc) into next ch-2 corner sp; rep from * twice more, ch 1, [work 3 dc into ch-1 sp, ch 1] 5 times, join with a sl st into top of beg ch-3. Sl st across the next 2 sts and into the corner sp.

RND 8: Ch 3, work (2 dc, ch 2, 3 dc) into corner sp, * ch 1, [work 3 dc into ch-1 sp, ch 1] 6 times, work (3 dc, ch 2, 3 dc) into next ch-2 corner sp; rep from * twice more, ch 1, [work 3 dc into ch-1 sp, ch 1] 6 times, join with a sl st into top of beg ch-3. Sl st across the next 2 sts and into the corner sp. Fasten off C.

RND 9: Join color B into any ch-2 corner sp, ch 3, work (2 dc, ch 2, 3 dc) into corner sp, * ch 1, [work 3 dc into ch-1 sp, ch 1] 7 times, work (3 dc, ch 2, 3 dc) into next ch-2 corner sp; rep from * twice more, ch 1, [work 3 dc into ch-1 sp, ch 1] 7 times, join with a sl st into top of beg ch-3. Sl st across the next 2 sts and into the corner sp.

RND 10: Ch 3, work (2 dc, ch 2, 3 dc) into corner sp, * ch 1, [work 3 dc into ch-1 sp, ch 1] 8 times, work (3 dc, ch 2, 3 dc) into next ch-2 corner sp; rep from * twice more, ch 1, [work 3 dc into ch-1 sp, ch 1] 8 times, join with a sl st into top of beg ch-3. Sl st across the next 2 sts and into the corner sp. Fasten off B.

RND 11: Join color A into any ch-2 corner sp, ch 3, work (2 dc, ch 2, 3 dc) into corner sp, * ch 1, [work 3 dc into ch-1 sp, ch 1] 9 times, work (3 dc, ch 2, 3 dc) into next ch-2 corner sp; rep from * twice more, ch 1, [work 3 dc into ch-1 sp, ch 1] 9 times, join with a sl st into top of beg ch-3. Sl st across the next 2 sts and into the corner sp.

RND 12: Ch 3, work (2 dc, ch 2, 3 dc) into corner sp, * ch 1, [work 3 dc into ch-1 sp, ch 1] 10 times, work (3 dc, ch 2, 3 dc) into next ch-2 corner sp; rep from * twice more, ch 1, [work 3 dc into ch-1 sp, ch 1] 10 times, join with a sl st into top of beg ch-3. Sl st across the next 2 sts and into the corner sp.

RND 13: Ch 3, work (2 dc, ch 2, 3 dc) into corner sp, * ch 1, [work 3 dc into ch-1 sp, ch 1] 11 times, work (3 dc, ch 2, 3 dc) into next ch-2 corner sp; rep from * twice more, ch 1, [work 3 dc into ch-1 sp, ch 1] 11 times, join with a sl st into top of beg ch-3. Sl st across the next 2 sts and into the corner sp.

RND 14: Ch 3, work (2 dc, ch 2, 3 dc) into corner sp, * ch 1, [work 3 dc into ch-1 sp, ch 1] 12 times, work (3 dc, ch 2, 3 dc) into next ch-2 corner sp; rep from * twice more, ch 1, [work 3 dc into ch-1 sp, ch 1] 12 times, join with a sl st into top of beg ch-3. Sl st across the next 2 sts and into the corner sp. Fasten off A.

RND 15: Join color C into any ch-2 corner sp, ch 3, work (2 dc, ch 2, 3 dc) into corner sp, * ch 1, [work 3 dc into ch-1 sp, ch 1] 13 times, work (3 dc, ch 2, 3 dc) into next ch-2 corner sp; rep from * twice more, ch 1, [work 3 dc into ch-1 sp, ch 1] 13 times, join with a sl st into top of beg ch-3. Sl st across the next 2 sts and into the corner sp.

RND 16: Ch 3, work (2 dc, ch 2, 3 dc) into corner sp, * ch 1, [work 3 dc into ch-1 sp, ch 1] 14 times, work (3 dc, ch 2, 3 dc) into next ch-2 corner sp; rep from * twice more, ch 1, [work 3 dc into ch-1 sp, ch 1] 14 times, join with a sl st into top of beg ch-3. Sl st across the next 2 sts and into the corner sp.

RND 17: Ch 3, work (2 dc, ch 2, 3 dc) into corner sp, * ch 1, [work 3 dc into ch-1 sp, ch 1] 15 times, work (3 dc, ch 2, 3 dc) into next ch-2 corner sp; rep from * twice more, ch 1, [work 3 dc into ch-1 sp, ch 1] 15 times, join with a sl st into top of beg ch-3. Sl st across the next 2 sts and into the corner sp. Fasten off C.

back

Work as for Front, changing colors as follows:

RNDS 1–16: Color D
RND 17: Color C

finishing

With RS of Front facing, sew buttons evenly spaced along one edge. Align Front and Back with WS facing, and with color C, join on three sides (leaving button side open) by working 1 sc in each ch-1 sp and dc and 3 sc in each ch-2 corner sp. On Back, opposite buttons, sc across, working ch 5 to create a button loop opposite each button. Fasten off C. Weave in ends. Block if desired. Insert pillow form. Close buttons.

Color Commentary from Sarah London

Yellow and orange has always been a favorite combination of mine. It's cheerful and warming. In this instance, I've injected a subtle touch of brown, which provides dimension while still retaining a radiating warmth. For the other cushion, red and pink blended with purple create a stately palette, balanced and harmonious.

Continue in pattern through Rnd 17 working 2 rnds with B, 4 rnds with A and 3 rnds with C.

giant floor cushion

A comfy, plump crocheted floor cushion provides extra casual seating in a hurry. Make a couple of these for when friends unexpectedly drop by or for storytime with your children. The stylish design of this fabulous soft seating will easily complement your decor.

yarn

5 skeins worsted weight yarn, 1 each of 3 colors (A, B and C) and 2 skeins of 1 color (D)

The cushion shown here was

made using Cascade 220 (100% Peruvian highland wool, 3.5oz/100g, 220yd/201m) in colors #9421 (A), #8339 (B), #7812 (C) and #9452 (D).

crochet hook

U.S. size G/6 (4mm)

notions

26" (66cm) square pillow form

9 buttons, ½" (13mm) diameter

Yarn needle

finished measurements

Approx. 26" (66cm) square

front

With color A, ch 5, join with a sl st to form a ring.

RND 1: Ch 3, work 2 dc into the ring, * ch 2, work 3 dc into the ring; rep from * twice more, ch 2, join with a sl st into top of beg ch-3. Sl st across the next 2 sts and into the corner sp.

RND 2: Ch 3, work (2 dc, ch 2, 3 dc) into corner sp, * ch 1, work (3 dc, ch 2, 3 dc) into next ch-2 corner sp; rep from * twice more, ch 1, join with a sl st into top of beg ch-3. Sl st across the next 2 sts and into the corner sp.

RND 3: Ch 3, work (2 dc, ch 2, 3 dc) into corner sp, * ch 1, work 3 dc into ch-1 sp, ch 1, work (3 dc, ch 2, 3 dc) into next ch-2 corner sp; rep from * twice more, ch 1, work 3 dc into ch-1 sp, ch 1, join with a sl st into top of beg ch-3. Sl st across the next 2 sts and into the corner sp.

RND 4: Ch 3, work (2 dc, ch 2, 3 dc) into corner sp, * ch 1, [work 3 dc into ch-1 sp, ch 1] twice, work (3 dc, ch 2, 3 dc) into next ch-2 corner sp; rep from * twice more, ch 1, [work 3 dc into ch-1 sp, ch 1] twice, join with a sl st into top of beg ch-3. Sl st across the next 2 sts and into the corner sp.

RND 5: Ch 3, work (2 dc, ch 2, 3 dc) into corner sp, * ch 1, [work 3 dc into ch-1 sp, ch 1] 3 times, work (3 dc, ch 2, 3 dc) into next ch-2 corner sp; rep from * twice more, ch 1, [work 3 dc into ch-1 sp, ch 1] 3 times, join with a sl st into top of beg ch-3. Sl st across the next 2 sts and into the corner sp.

RND 6: Ch 3, work (2 dc, ch 2, 3 dc) into corner sp, * ch 1, [work 3 dc into ch-1 sp, ch 1] 4 times, work (3 dc, ch 2, 3 dc) into next ch-2 corner sp; rep from * twice more, ch 1, [work 3 dc into ch-1 sp, ch 1] 4 times, join with a sl st into top of beg ch-3. Sl st across the next 2 sts and into the corner sp.

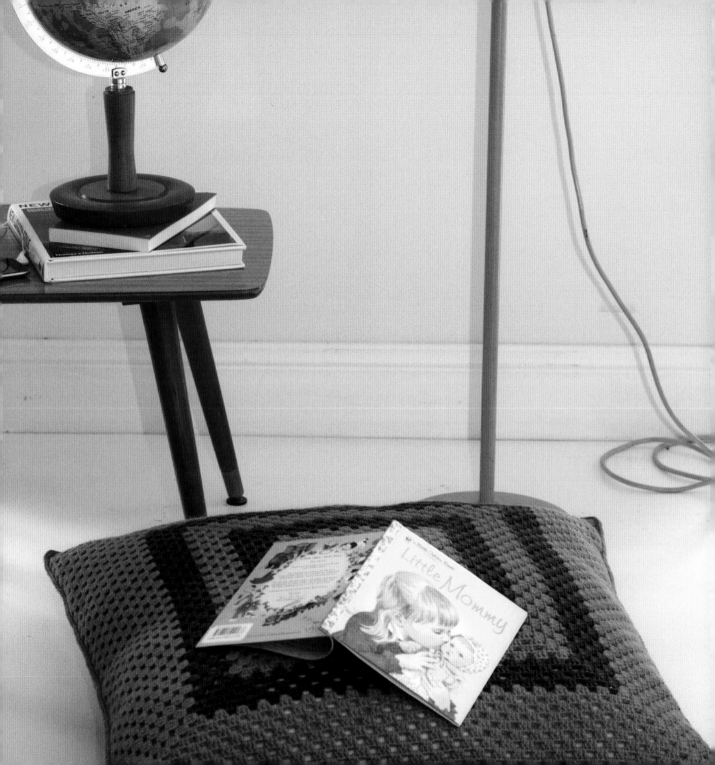

RND 7: Ch 3, work (2 dc, ch 2, 3 dc) into corner sp, * ch 1, [work 3 dc into ch-1 sp, ch 1] 5 times, work (3 dc, ch 2, 3 dc) into next ch-2 corner sp; rep from * twice more, ch 1, [work 3 dc into ch-1 sp, ch 1] 5 times, join with a sl st into top of beg ch-3. Sl st across the next 2 sts and into the corner sp.

RND 8: Ch 3, work (2 dc, ch 2, 3 dc) into corner sp, * ch 1, [work 3 dc into ch-1 sp, ch 1] 6 times, work (3 dc, ch 2, 3 dc) into next ch-2 corner sp; rep from * twice more, ch 1, [work 3 dc into ch-1 sp, ch 1] 6 times, join with a sl st into top of beg ch-3. Sl st across the next 2 sts and into the corner sp. Fasten off A.

For the remainder of the cushion, work in granny square patt as set, changing colors as follows:

RNDS 9–12: Color B

RNDS 13–16: Color C

RNDS 17–20: Color B

RNDS 21–28: Color A

RNDS 29–31: Color C

back

Work as for Front, using color D throughout.

finishing

With RS of Front facing, sew buttons evenly spaced along one edge. Align Front and Back with WS facing, and with color C, join on three sides (leaving button side open) by working 1 sc in each ch-1 sp and dc and 3 sc in each ch-2 corner sp. On Back, opposite buttons, sc across, working ch 5 to create a button loop opposite each button. Fasten off. Weave in ends. Block if desired. Insert pillow form. Close buttons.

Color Commentary from Sarah London

Floor cushions are ideal for introducing color into a room. They inject a little quirkiness and can be added or subtracted when required, so they do not necessarily have to match perfectly with the other color components of the room. Some say green and blue should never be seen together—what nonsense! I personally love green and blue combined. Inspired by the colors of the sea, this giant granny square cushion fuses the colors beautifully. A deeper blue gives the cushion foundation.

Continue in pattern through Rnd 31 working 4 rnds each with B, C and B, 8 rnds with A and 3 rnds with C.

lampshade cover

Turn drab into fab! Cover an outdated drum lampshade with a nifty tube of crocheted granny squares. You will be surprised and delighted with the outcome. Your refashioned lampshade will instantly brighten and freshen any corner of your living room and will provide a lovely, soft glow of light.

yarn

5 skeins worsted weight yarn, 1 each of 3 colors (A, B and C) and 2 skeins of 1 color (D)

The lampshade cover shown here was made using Cascade 220 (100% Peruvian highland wool, 3.5oz/100g, 220yd/201m) in colors #7804 (A), #8894 (B), #8408 (C) and #8010 (D).

crochet hook

U.S. size G/6 (4mm)

notions

Drum lampshade; 15" (38cm) diameter × 11" (28cm) tall

Yarn needle

Sewing needle

Clear monofilament thread

finished measurements

Approx. 42" × 11" (106.5cm × 28cm) before joining into a tube

square

Make 16.

With color A, ch 5, join with a sl st to form a ring.

RND 1: Ch 3, work 2 dc into the ring, * ch 2, work 3 dc into the ring; rep from * twice more, ch 2, join with a sl st into top of beg ch-3. Sl st across the next 2 sts and into the corner sp. Fasten off A.

RND 2: Join color D into any ch-2 corner sp, ch 3, work (2 dc, ch 2, 3 dc) into corner sp, * ch 1, work (3 dc, ch 2, 3 dc) into next ch-2 corner sp; rep from * twice more, ch 1, join with a sl st into top of beg ch-3. Sl st across the next 2 sts and into the corner sp. Fasten off D.

RND 3: Join color B into any ch-2 corner sp, ch 3, work (2 dc, ch 2, 3 dc) into corner sp, * ch 1, work 3 dc into ch-1 sp, ch 1, work (3 dc, ch 2, 3 dc) into next ch-2 corner sp; rep from * twice more, ch 1, work 3 dc into ch-1 sp, ch 1, join with a sl st into top of beg ch-3. Sl st across the next 2 sts and into the corner sp.

RND 4: Ch 3, work (2 dc, ch 2, 3 dc) into corner sp, * ch 1, [work 3 dc into ch-1 sp, ch 1] twice, work (3 dc, ch 2, 3 dc) into next ch-2 corner sp; rep from * twice more, ch 1, [work 3 dc into ch-1 sp, ch 1] twice, join with a sl st into top of beg ch-3. Sl st across the next 2 sts and into the corner sp. Fasten off B.

RND 5: Join color C into any ch-2 corner sp, ch 3, work (2 dc, ch 2, 3 dc) into corner sp, * ch 1, [work 3 dc into ch-1 sp, ch 1] 3 times, work (3 dc, ch 2, 3 dc) into next ch-2 corner sp; rep from * twice more, ch 1, [work 3 dc into ch-1 sp, ch 1] 3 times, join with a sl st into top of beg ch-3. Sl st across the next 2 sts and into the corner sp. Fasten off C.

RND 6: Join color D into any ch-2 corner sp, ch 3, work (2 dc, ch 2, 3 dc) into corner sp, * ch 1, [work 3 dc into ch-1 sp, ch 1] 4 times, work (3 dc, ch 2, 3 dc) into next ch-2 corner sp; rep from * twice more, ch 1, [work 3 dc into ch-1 sp, ch 1] 4 times, join with a sl st into top of beg ch-3. Sl st across the next 2 sts and into the corner sp. Fasten off D.

finishing

Join squares in 2 rows of 8 squares each using your preferred method. Join the ends to form a tube.

EDGING

RND 1: Join color D into any ch-1 sp, ch 3, work 2 dc into same sp, * ch 1, work 3 dc into next ch-1 sp; rep from * around, ch 1, join with a sl st into top of beg ch-3.

RND 2: Ch 3, work 1 dc into each st and ch-1 sp around, join with a sl st into top of beg ch-3. Fasten off D.

Weave in ends. Block if desired. Place tube over lampshade. With sewing needle and monofilament thread, stitch in place.

Color Commentary from Sarah London

With a neutral base of cream as the foundation, a palette of pink, green and brown unite to create a pleasing combination. Green and brown are quite earthy, so I added a slight splattering of rosy pink to lift the palette. The colors have been kept to a bare minimum with this project to allow the other crocheted items of the living room to take center stage. Floor lamps are usually positioned close to the sofa—if you're piling your sofa with colorful crocheted cushions, it is probably best to minimize the palette when making a lampshade cover.

ottoman slipcover

An ottoman is a multifunctional piece of furniture that no living room should be without. It can provide extra storage and seating in your living room and may even be used as a coffee table. Transform an existing ottoman or a simple square cube with bands of crocheted color. This stylish slipcover will help your ottoman take center stage!

yarn

8 skeins worsted weight yarn, 1 each of 8 colors (A, B, C, D, E, F, G and H)

The slipcover shown here was made using Cascade 220 (100% Peruvian highland wool, 3.5oz/100g, 220yd/201m) in colors #9473 (A), #9541 (B), #7808 (C), #9492 (D), #8686 (E), #2415 (F), #8339 (G) and #8415 (H).

crochet hook

U.S. size G/6 (4mm)

notions

15½" (39.5cm) cube ottoman

Yarn needle

finished measurements

Approx. 15½" (39.5cm) cube

With color A, ch 5, join with a sl st to form a ring.

RND 1: Ch 3, work 2 dc into the ring, * ch 2, work 3 dc into the ring; rep from * twice more, ch 2, join with a sl st into top of beg ch-3. Sl st across the next 2 sts and into the corner sp.

RND 2: Ch 3, work (2 dc, ch 2, 3 dc) into corner sp, * ch 1, work (3 dc, ch 2, 3 dc) into next ch-2 corner sp; rep from * twice more, ch 1, join with a sl st into top of beg ch-3. Sl st across the next 2 sts and into the corner sp.

RND 3: Ch 3, work (2 dc, ch 2, 3 dc) into corner sp, * ch 1, work 3 dc into ch-1 sp, ch 1, work (3 dc, ch 2, 3 dc) into next ch-2 corner sp; rep from * twice more, ch 1, work 3 dc into ch-1 sp, ch 1, join with a sl st into top of beg ch-3. Sl st across the next 2 sts and into the corner sp.

RND 4: Ch 3, work (2 dc, ch 2, 3 dc) into corner sp, * ch 1, [work 3 dc into ch-1 sp, ch 1] twice, work (3 dc, ch 2, 3 dc) into next ch-2 corner sp; rep from * twice more, ch 1, [work 3 dc into ch-1 sp, ch 1] twice, join with a sl st into top of beg ch-3. Sl st across the next 2 sts and into the corner sp.

RND 5: Ch 3, work (2 dc, ch 2, 3 dc) into corner sp, * ch 1, [work 3 dc into ch-1 sp, ch 1] 3 times, work (3 dc, ch 2, 3 dc) into next ch-2 corner sp; rep from * twice more, ch 1, [work 3 dc into ch-1 sp, ch 1] 3 times, join with a sl st into top of beg ch-3. Sl st across the next 2 sts and into the corner sp.

RND 6: Ch 3, work (2 dc, ch 2, 3 dc) into corner sp, * ch 1, [work 3 dc into ch-1 sp, ch 1] 4 times, work (3 dc, ch 2, 3 dc) into next ch-2 corner sp; rep from * twice more, ch 1, [work 3 dc into ch-1 sp, ch 1] 4 times, join with a sl st into top of beg ch-3. Sl st across the next 2 sts and into the corner sp.

RND 7: Ch 3, work (2 dc, ch 2, 3 dc) into corner sp, * ch 1, [work 3 dc into ch-1 sp, ch 1] 5 times, work (3 dc, ch 2, 3 dc) into next ch-2 corner sp; rep from * twice more, ch 1, [work 3 dc into ch-1 sp, ch 1] 5 times, join with a sl st into top of beg ch-3. Sl st across the next 2 sts and into the corner sp.

RND 8: Ch 3, work (2 dc, ch 2, 3 dc) into corner sp, * ch 1, [work 3 dc into ch-1 sp, ch 1] 6 times, work (3 dc, ch 2, 3 dc) into next ch-2 corner sp; rep from * twice more, ch 1, [work 3 dc into ch-1 sp, ch 1] 6 times, join with a sl st into top of beg ch-3. Sl st across the next 2 sts and into the corner sp. Fasten off A.

RNDS 9–13: With color B, work in granny square patt as set. At the end of Rnd 13, fasten off B.

RNDS 14–18: With color C, work in granny square patt as set. At the end of Rnd 18, fasten off C.

Note: At this point, the top of the slipcover is complete and the sides will now be formed.

RND 19: Join color D into any ch-2 corner sp, ch 3, work 2 dc into corner sp, * ch 1, work 3 dc into next sp; rep from * around, working 3 dc into each ch-1 sp and ch-2 corner sp, join with a sl st into top of beg ch-3. Sl st across the next 2 sts and into the next ch-1 sp.

RND 20: Ch 3, work 2 dc into ch-1 sp, * ch 1, work 3 dc into next ch-1 sp; rep from * around, join with a sl st into top of beg ch-3. Sl st across the next 2 sts and into the next ch-1 sp.

RNDS 21–26: With color D, work as for Rnd 20. At the end of Rnd 26, fasten off D.

RNDS 27–34: With color E, work as for Rnd 20. At the end of Rnd 34, fasten off E.

RNDS 35–42: With color F, work as for Rnd 20. At the end of Rnd 42, fasten off F.

RNDS 43–50: With color G, work as for Rnd 20. At the end of Rnd 50, fasten off G.

RNDS 51–58: With color H, work as for Rnd 20. At the end of Rnd 58, fasten off H.

finishing

Weave in ends. Block if desired. Place slipcover over ottoman.

Color Commentary from Sarah London

A range of darker colors was chosen for this project. Charcoal, purples, apricot, chocolate, mustard, blue and burgundy meld together nicely. The bands of deep, masculine color make a visual statement in a living room and are perfectly suited to combine with a sofa in a deep color, particularly mustard or maroon.

Continue in pattern working 8 rnds
each with D, E, F, G and H.

Continue in pattern through Rnd 18 working 5 rnds each with B and C.

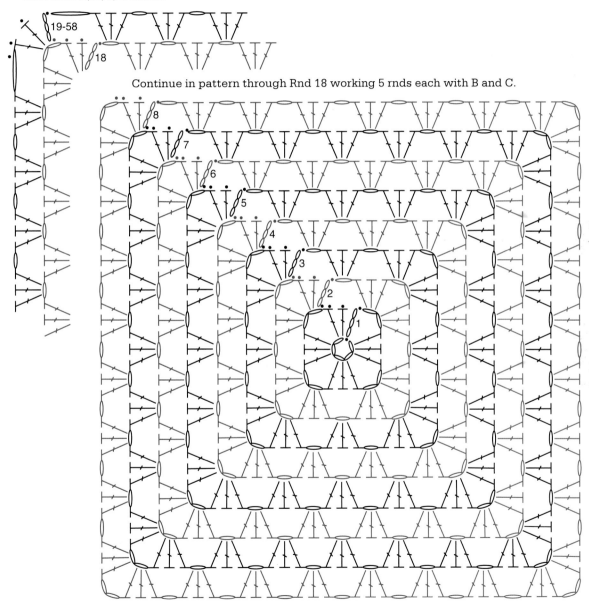

sofa blanket

Boldly make a color impact with a sprightly granny square blanket. This lively multicolored blanket will brighten any living room and fill it with sunshine even on the grayest of days. When the weather turns chilly, keep your blanket close at hand by draping it over the back of the sofa. A crocheted granny square blanket will provide comfort and warmth on chilly winter evenings and will be loved by many generations.

yarn

Worsted weight yarn in a random assortment of colors (small amounts are okay); each square uses approx. 38yds (35m) of yarn

The blanket shown here was made using Cascade 220 (100% Peruvian highland wool, 3.5oz/100g, 220yd/201m).

crochet hook

U.S. size G/6 (4mm)

notions

Yarn needle

finished measurements

As desired; each square measures 6" × 6" (15cm × 15cm)

square

Make number desired.

With desired color, ch 5, join with a sl st to form a ring.

RND 1: Ch 3, work 2 dc into the ring, * ch 2, work 3 dc into the ring; rep from * twice more, ch 2, join with a sl st into top of beg ch-3. Sl st across the next 2 sts and into the corner sp.

RND 2: Ch 3, work (2 dc, ch 2, 3 dc) into corner sp, * ch 1, work (3 dc, ch 2, 3 dc) into next ch-2 corner sp; rep from * twice more, ch 1, join with a sl st into top of beg ch-3. Sl st across the next 2 sts and into the corner sp. Fasten off current color.

RND 3: Join new color into any ch-2 corner sp, ch 3, work (2 dc, ch 2, 3 dc) into corner sp, * ch 1, work 3 dc into ch-1 sp, ch 1, work (3 dc, ch 2, 3 dc) into next ch-2 corner sp; rep from * twice more, ch 1, work 3 dc into ch-1 sp, ch 1, join with a sl st into top of beg ch-3. Sl st across the next 2 sts and into the corner sp. Fasten off current color.

RND 4: Join new color into any ch-2 corner sp, ch 3, work (2 dc, ch 2, 3 dc) into corner sp, * ch 1, [work 3 dc into ch-1 sp, ch 1] twice, work (3 dc, ch 2, 3 dc) into next ch-2 corner sp; rep from * twice more, ch 1, [work 3 dc into ch-1 sp, ch 1] twice, join with a sl st into top of beg ch-3. Sl st across the next 2 sts and into the corner sp. Fasten off current color.

RND 5: Join new color into any ch-2 corner sp, ch 3, work (2 dc, ch 2, 3 dc) into corner sp, * ch 1, [work 3 dc into ch-1 sp, ch 1] 3 times, work (3 dc, ch 2, 3 dc) into next ch-2 corner sp; rep from * twice more, ch 1, [work 3 dc into ch-1 sp, ch 1] 3 times, join with a sl st into top of beg ch-3. Sl st across the next 2 sts and into the corner sp. Fasten off current color.

RND 6: Join new color into any ch-2 corner sp, ch 3, work (2 dc, ch 2, 3 dc) into corner sp, * ch 1, [work 3 dc into ch-1 sp, ch 1] 4 times, work (3 dc, ch 2, 3 dc) into next ch-2 corner sp; rep from * twice more, ch 1, [work 3 dc into ch-1 sp, ch 1] 4 times, join with a sl st into top of beg ch-3. Sl st across the next 2 sts and into the corner sp.

RND 7: Ch 3, work (2 dc, ch 2, 3 dc) into corner sp, * ch 1, [work 3 dc into ch-1 sp, ch 1] 5 times, work (3 dc, ch 2, 3 dc) into next ch-2 corner sp; rep from * twice more, ch 1, [work 3 dc into ch-1 sp, ch 1] 5 times, join with a sl st into top of beg ch-3. Sl st across the next 2 sts and into the corner sp. Fasten off current color.

finishing

Join squares using preferred method. Weave in ends. Block if desired.

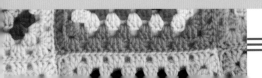

Color Commentary from Sarah London

My method for making a multicolored granny square blanket is simple—more is more. Collect as many colors as possible to create a captivating blanket saturated in color. I work in a somewhat production-line fashion on a blanket like this. First I crochet the first two rounds for every square, incorporating every color from my collection of yarn. It's not necessary to overanalyze color components when making multicolored blankets; randomly chosen colors ignite their own special magic. Continue randomly adding colored rounds to each square. When I work, often the next color added will be the color closest to me. Have fun with color and you won't go wrong.

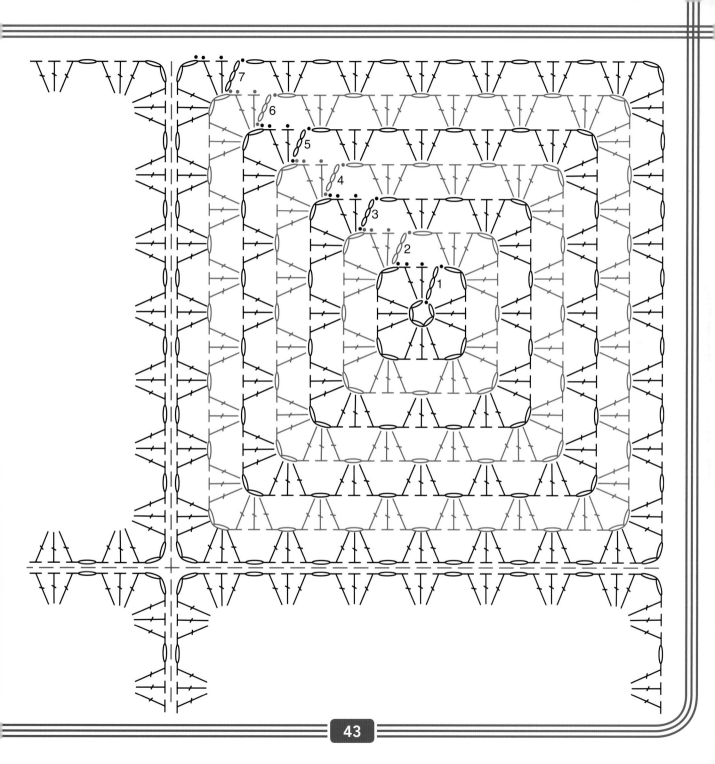

christmas stocking

When Christmas Eve arrives, nothing is more exciting for children (and some adults!) than hanging their stockings above the fireplace. The anticipation of waking on Christmas morning to find a stocking filled with gifts, candy and toys is a memory to last a lifetime. Make a roomy Christmas stocking for each member of your family—it will be enjoyed and cherished for many Christmases to come.

yarn

1 skein worsted weight yarn (A)

Small amounts of worsted weight yarn in 3 colors (B, C and D)

The stockings shown here were made using Cascade 220 (100% Peruvian highland wool, 3.5oz/100g, 220yd/201m). Stocking 1 uses colors #8894 (A), #9541 (B), #7828 (C) and #7804 (D). Stocking 2 uses colors #7812 (A), #9470 (B), #7830 (C) and #8908 (D).

crochet hook

U.S. size H/8 (5mm)

notions

Yarn needle

finished measurements

Approx. 16" (40.5cm) long

hexagon

Make 1.

With color A, ch 5, join with a sl st to form a ring.

RND 1: Ch 3, work 2 dc into the ring, * ch 2, work 3 dc into the ring; rep from * 4 times more, ch 2, join with a sl st into top of beg ch-3. Sl st across the next 2 sts and into the corner sp.

RND 2: Ch 3, work (2 dc, ch 2, 3 dc) into corner sp, * ch 1, work (3 dc, ch 2, 3 dc) into next ch-2 corner sp; rep from * 4 times more, ch 1, join with a sl st into top of beg ch-3. Sl st across the next 2 sts and into the corner sp.

RND 3: Ch 3, work (2 dc, ch 2, 3 dc) into corner sp, * ch 1, work 3 dc into ch-1 sp, ch 1, work (3 dc, ch 2, 3 dc) into next ch-2 corner sp; rep from * 4 times more, ch 1, work 3 dc into ch-1 sp, ch 1, join with a sl st into top of beg ch-3. Sl st across the next 2 sts and into the corner sp.

RND 4: Ch 3, work (2 dc, ch 2, 3 dc) into corner sp, * ch 1, [work 3 dc into ch-1 sp, ch 1] twice, work (3 dc, ch 2, 3 dc) into next ch-2 corner sp; rep from * 4 times more, ch 1, [work 3 dc into ch-1 sp, ch 1] twice, join with a sl st into top of beg ch-3. Sl st across the next 2 sts and into the corner sp.

RND 5: Ch 3, work (2 dc, ch 2, 3 dc) into corner sp, * ch 1, [work 3 dc into ch-1 sp, ch 1] 3 times, work (3 dc, ch 2, 3 dc) into next ch-2 corner sp; rep from * 4 times more, ch 1, [work 3 dc into ch-1 sp, ch 1] 3 times, join with a sl st into top of beg ch-3. Sl st across the next 2 sts and into the corner sp.

RND 6: Ch 3, work (2 dc, ch 2, 3 dc) into corner sp, * ch 1, [work 3 dc into ch-1 sp, ch 1] 4 times, work (3 dc, ch 2, 3 dc) into next ch-2 corner sp; rep from * 4 times more, ch 1, [work 3 dc into ch-1 sp, ch 1] 4 times, join with a sl st into top of beg ch-3. Sl st across the next 2 sts and into the corner sp.

RND 7: Ch 3, work (2 dc, ch 2, 3 dc) into corner sp, * ch 1, [work 3 dc into ch-1 sp, ch 1] 5 times, work (3 dc, ch 2, 3 dc) into next ch-2 corner sp; rep from * 4 times more, ch 1, [work 3 dc into ch-1 sp, ch 1] 5 times, join with a sl st into top of beg ch-3. Sl st across the next 2 sts and into the corner sp.

RND 8: Ch 3, work (2 dc, ch 2, 3 dc) into corner sp, * ch 1, [work 3 dc into ch-1 sp, ch 1] 6 times, work (3 dc, ch 2, 3 dc) into next ch-2 corner sp; rep from * 4 times more, ch 1, [work 3 dc into ch-1 sp, ch 1] 6 times, join with a sl st into top of beg ch-3. Sl st across the next 2 sts and into the corner sp.

RND 9: Ch 3, work (2 dc, ch 2, 3 dc) into corner sp, * ch 1, [work 3 dc into ch-1 sp, ch 1] 7 times, work (3 dc, ch 2, 3 dc) into next ch-2 corner sp; rep from * 4 times more, ch 1, [work 3 dc into ch-1 sp, ch 1] 7 times, join with a sl st into top of beg ch-3. Sl st across the next 2 sts and into the corner sp.

RND 10: Ch 3, work (2 dc, ch 2, 3 dc) into corner sp, * ch 1, [work 3 dc into ch-1 sp, ch 1] 8 times, work (3 dc, ch 2, 3 dc) into next ch-2 corner sp; rep from * 4 times more, ch 1, [work 3 dc into ch-1 sp, ch 1] 8 times, join with a sl st into top of beg ch-3. Sl st across the next 2 sts and into the corner sp. Fasten off A.

With RS facing, fold the Hexagon in half to form an L shape. With color A, join the Hexagon along the two long sides with a row of sc, leaving the top and bottom edges open. Turn to RS.

leg

RND 1: Join color A into any ch-1 sp at the top opening of the Hexagon, ch 3, work 2 dc into same sp, * ch 1, work 3 dc into next ch-1 sp; rep from * around, ch 1, join with a sl st into top of beg ch-3. Sl st across the next 2 sts and into the next ch-1 sp.

RNDS 2–10: Ch 3, work 2 dc into same sp, * ch 1, work 3 dc into next ch-1 sp; rep from * around, ch 1, join with a sl st into top of beg ch-3. Sl st across the next 2 sts and into the next ch-1 sp. Fasten off A at end of Rnd 10.

RND 11: Join color B into any ch-1 sp, ch 3, work 2 dc into same sp, * ch 1, work 3 dc into next ch-1 sp; rep from * around, ch 1, join with a sl st into top of beg ch-3. Sl st across the next 2 sts and into the next ch-1 sp. Fasten off B.

RND 12: Join color C into any ch-1 sp, ch 3, work 2 dc into same sp, * ch 1, work 3 dc into next ch-1 sp; rep from * around, ch 1, join with a sl st into top of beg ch-3. Sl st across the next 2 sts and into the next ch-1 sp. Fasten off C.

RND 13: Join color D into any ch-1 sp, ch 3, work 2 dc into same sp, * ch 1, work 3 dc into next ch-1 sp; rep from * around, ch 1, join with a sl st into top of beg ch-3. Sl st across the next 2 sts and into the next ch-1 sp. Fasten off D.

RND 14: Join color A into any ch-1 sp, ch 3, work 2 dc into same sp, * ch 1, work 3 dc into next ch-1 sp; rep from * around, ch 1, join with a sl st into top of beg ch-3. Sl st across the next 2 sts and into the next ch-1 sp. Fasten off A.

toe

RND 1: Working on opposite open end of Hexagon, join color A into any ch-1 sp, ch 2, work 1 hdc into each ch-1 sp and dc around, join with a sl st into top of beg ch-2.

RND 2: Ch 3, [work 3 dc tog] around, join with a sl st.

RND 3: Ch 3, [work 3 dc tog] around, join with a sl st. Fasten off.

loop

Join color A into ch-1 sp at the back of the Leg along top edge of stocking, ch 8, sc into next ch-1 sp. Fasten off.

finishing

Weave in ends. Block if desired.

Color Commentary from Sarah London

Traditionally green and red are the favored colors for the Christmas season. I've selected green to form these Christmas stockings, brightening each stocking with a few rows of everyday color. With an overdose of red around our homes at Christmastime, green stockings make for a refreshing change.

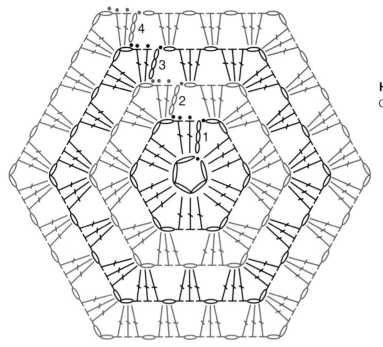

Hexagon
Continue in pattern through Rnd 10.

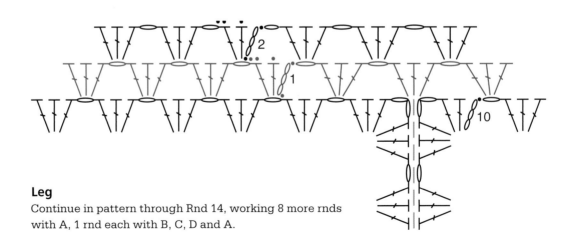

Leg
Continue in pattern through Rnd 14, working 8 more rnds with A, 1 rnd each with B, C, D and A.

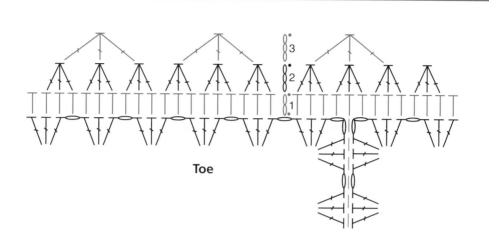

Toe

chapter three

The Kitchen

Step into the most utilitarian room of the house in this chapter and find lively ways to brighten your kitchen with crochet. Each project will inject a splash of color, giving you a bright, cheerful kitchen. The first project is a slipcover crocheted in rounds of color to quickly update a plain kitchen stool. I love slipcovers because they are easily removed for laundering when spills occur. You can coordinate the color of your slipcover with the other accessories in your kitchen to give a clean, fresh look to the room. A stool isn't the only thing you can update in this chapter: Modernize a thrifted vintage apron with a nifty granny square pocket. As well as being a dream to wear when baking, this apron will look just as nice hanging on a hook when not in use, adding an extra burst of color to your kitchen.

The projects in this chapter aren't just pretty, though—they're hardworking, too. Try stitching a practical dishcloth to scrub your dishes clean. Working in a closely woven pattern ensures that your dishcloths will be long wearing. Dishcloths make super gifts, too, so make a few extra and pop them in a gift draw for future occasions. Next is a pot holder that will not only protect your hands, but also add an artful touch to the kitchen in an instant! Pot holders are especially suitable as a beginner's project when you are just starting out on your crochet adventure. The simple Pot Holder pattern on page 62 will allow you to experiment with various color combinations while learning to crochet. The last project in this chapter, the Grocer's Tote on page 66, is perfect for running errands about town. I'll show you how to transform an ordinary, environmentally friendly tote into a colorful head-turner in no time at all!

stool cover

A stool is a handy piece of furniture for the kitchen. A pretty slipcover crocheted in rounds can update a tired stool in an instant and will also inject some color into an otherwise drab kitchen. The beauty of a slipcover is that it is practical as well as pretty—it can be easily removed for laundering. This cover is a welcome accessory to a well-dressed kitchen.

yarn

4 skeins worsted weight yarn, 1 each of 4 colors (A, B, C and D)

The stool cover shown here was made using Cascade 220 (100% Peruvian highland wool, 3.5oz/100g, 220yd/201m) in colors #9473 (A), #8914 (B), #4192 (C) and #8339 (D).

crochet hook

U.S. size G/6 (4mm)

notions

Yarn needle

finished measurements

Approx. 12" (30.5cm) diameter

RND 1: With color A, ch 4, work 11 dc into 4th ch from hook, join with a sl st into top of beg ch-3.

RND 2: Ch 3, work 1 dc into same st, * ch 1, work 2 dc into next st; rep from * around, ch 1, join with a sl st into top of beg ch-3. Sl st into the next stitch and into the ch-1 sp. Fasten off A.

RND 3: Join color B into any ch-1 sp, ch 3, work 2 dc into same sp, * ch 1, work 3 dc into next ch-1 sp; rep from * around, ch 1, join with a sl st into top of beg ch-3. Sl st across the next 2 sts and into the ch-1 sp.

RND 4: Ch 3, work 2 dc into same sp, * ch 1, work 3 dc into next ch-1 sp; rep from * around, ch 1, join with a sl st into top of beg ch-3. Sl st across the next 2 sts and into the ch-1 sp. Fasten off B.

RND 5: Join color C into any ch-1 sp, ch 3, work 2 dc into same sp, * ch 2, work 3 dc into next ch-1 sp; rep from * around, ch 2, join with a sl st into top of beg ch-3. Sl st across the next 2 sts and into the ch-2 sp. Fasten off C.

RND 6: Join color A into any ch-2 sp, ch 3, work (1 dc, ch 1, 2 dc) into same sp, * ch 1, work (2 dc, ch 1, 2 dc) into next ch-2 sp; rep from * around, ch 1, join with a sl st into top of beg ch-3. Sl st into the next st and into the ch-1 sp.

RND 7: Ch 3, work 2 dc into same sp, * ch 1, work 3 dc into next ch-1 sp; rep from * around, ch 1, join with a sl st into top of beg ch-3. Sl st across the next 2 sts and into the ch-1 sp. Fasten off A.

RND 8: Join color D into any ch-1 sp, ch 3, work 2 dc into same sp, * ch 1, work 3 dc into next ch-1 sp; rep from * around, ch 1, join with a sl st into top of beg ch-3. Sl st across the next 2 sts and into the ch-1 sp. Fasten off D.

RND 9: Join color B into any ch-1 sp, ch 3, work 2 dc into same sp, * ch 2, work 3 dc into next ch-1 sp; rep from * around, ch 2, join with a sl st into top of beg ch-3. Sl st across the next 2 sts and into the ch-2 sp.

RND 10: Ch 3, work (1 dc, ch 1, 2 dc) into same sp, * ch 1, work (2 dc, ch 1, 2 dc) into next ch-2 sp; rep from * around, ch 1, join with a sl st into top of beg ch-3. Sl st into the next st and into the ch-1 sp. Fasten off B.

RND 11: Join color C into any ch-1 sp, ch 3, work 1 dc into same sp, * ch 1, work 2 dc into next ch-1 sp; rep from * around, ch 1, join with a sl st into top of beg ch-3. Sl st into the next stitch and into the ch-1 sp. Fasten off C.

RND 12: Join color D into any ch-1 sp, ch 3, work 1 dc into each st and ch around, join with a sl st into top of beg ch-3. Fasten off D.

RND 13: Join color C into any st, ch 3, work 1 dc into each st around, join with a sl st into top of beg ch-3.

RND 14: Ch 3, work 1 dc into each st around, join with a sl st into top of beg ch-3.

RND 15: Ch 2, work 1 hdc into each st around, join with a sl st into top of beg ch-2. Fasten off C.

finishing

Weave in ends. Block if desired. Stretch over top of stool.

Color Commentary from Sarah London

Crocheted rounds of charcoal, olive, lilac and petrol blue combine in a circular formation. Charcoal and petrol blue form a strong composition, while lilac and olive soften the palette. Color inspiration can be drawn from your kitchen curtains when making this project if you prefer your stool cover to match the room. I find, though, that a little clashing of colors makes for a more interesting room.

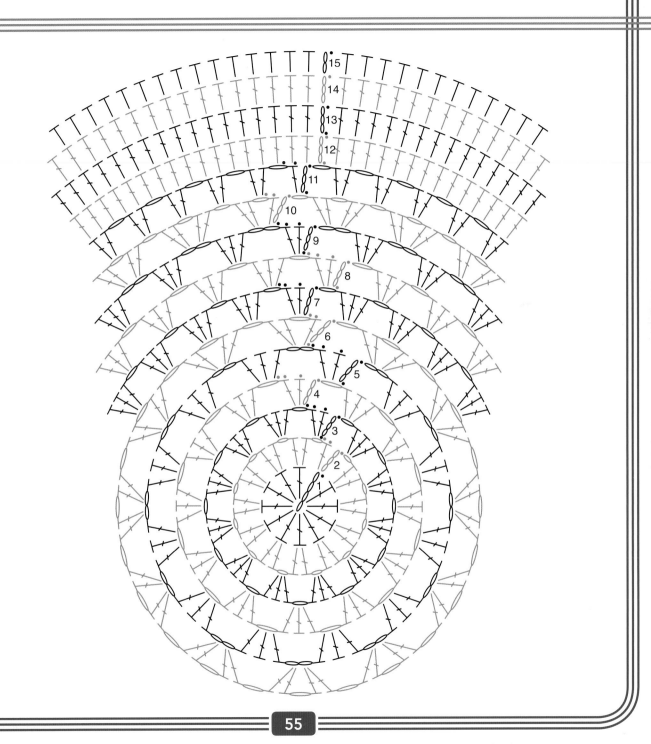

apron pocket

An apron is an essential element in my kitchen, and an apron with a roomy pocket is even more welcome. Three adventurously colored granny squares make a pocket that can be effortlessly attached to the front of a thrifted vintage apron. This easy addition creates a very special, unique apron.

yarn

Worsted weight yarn in a random assortment of colors (small amounts are okay), 5 colors for each square (A, B, C, D and E), plus 1 color for edging (F); a total of approx. 25yds (23m) of yarn is required

The apron pocket shown here was made using Cascade 220 (100% Peruvian highland wool, 3.5oz/100g, 220yd/201m). Square 1 uses colors #8408 (A), #7830 (B), #9469 (C), #8412 (D) and #9477 (E). Square 2 uses colors #7804 (A), #8412 (B), #7828 (C), #8905 (D) and #8509 (E). Square 3 uses colors #9470 (A), #9484 (B), #9493 (C), #9542 (D) and #9076 (E). The edging uses color #8894 (F).

crochet hook

Size U.S. G/6 (4mm)

notions

Vintage apron

Yarn needle

Sewing needle

Clear monofilament thread

finished measurements

Pocket: Approx. 13½" × 4½" (34.5cm × 11.5cm)

square

Make 3.

With color A, ch 5, join with a sl st to form a ring.

RND 1: Ch 3, work 2 dc into the ring, * ch 2, work 3 dc into the ring; rep from * twice more, ch 2, join with a sl st into top of beg ch-3. Sl st across the next 2 sts and into the corner sp. Fasten off A.

RND 2: Join color B into any ch-2 corner sp, ch 3, work (2 dc, ch 2, 3 dc) into corner sp, * ch 1, work (3 dc, ch 2, 3 dc) into next ch-2 corner sp; rep from * twice more, ch 1, join with a sl st into top of beg ch-3. Sl st across the next 2 sts and into the corner sp. Fasten off B.

RND 3: Join color C into any ch-2 corner sp, ch 3, work (2 dc, ch 2, 3 dc) into corner sp, * ch 1, work 3 dc into ch-1 sp, ch 1, work (3 dc, ch 2, 3 dc) into next ch-2 corner sp; rep from * twice more, ch 1, work 3 dc into ch-1 sp, ch 1, join with a sl st into top of beg ch-3. Sl st across the next 2 sts and into the corner sp. Fasten off C.

RND 4: Join color D into any ch-2 corner sp, ch 3, work (2 dc, ch 2, 3 dc) into corner sp, * ch 1, [work 3 dc into ch-1 sp, ch 1] twice, work (3 dc, ch 2, 3 dc) into next ch-2 corner sp; rep from * twice more, ch 1, [work 3 dc into ch-1 sp, ch 1] twice, join with a sl st into top of beg ch-3. Sl st across the next 2 sts and into the corner sp. Fasten off D.

RND 5: Join color E into any ch-2 corner sp, ch 3, work (2 dc, ch 2, 3 dc) into corner sp, * ch 1, [work 3 dc into ch-1 sp, ch 1] 3 times, work (3 dc, ch 2, 3 dc) into next ch-2 corner sp; rep from * twice more, ch 1, [work 3 dc into ch-1 sp, ch 1] 3 times, join with a sl st into top of beg ch-3. Sl st across the next 2 sts and into the corner sp. Fasten off E.

finishing

Join squares in a strip using preferred method.

EDGING (WORK AROUND STRIP)

NEXT RND: Join color F into any ch-2 corner sp, ch 2, work (1 hdc, ch 2, 2 hdc) into same sp, work 1 hdc into each st and ch around, working (2 hdc, ch 2, 2 hdc) into each ch-2 corner sp.

Weave in ends. Block if desired. With sewing needle and monofilament thread, stitch pocket onto the center front of the apron, leaving the top edge open.

Color Commentary from Sarah London

Orphan granny squares made from a mixture of colors combine to form a practical pocket on a vintage apron. Trim your pocket with a color extracted from your own thrifted apron to tie the colors together.

dishcloth

Brightly colored dishcloths make a statement in any kitchen and make washing the dishes and cleaning up spills a breeze. Functionality is key, so it is important to work dishcloths in a crochet stitch with a tight gauge; this will make your dishcloth last and maintain its shape. Making a stack of brightly colored dishcloths is a quick and easy way to add color to your kitchen sink.

yarn

1 skein worsted weight yarn

The dishcloths shown here were made using Cascade 220 (100% Peruvian highland wool, 3.5oz/100g, 220yd/201m). Dishcloth 1 uses color #9542. Dishcloth 2 uses color #8901.

crochet hook

U.S. size G/6 (4mm)

notions

Yarn needle

finished measurements

Approx. 7" × 9" (18cm × 23cm)

Ch 29.

ROW 1: Work 1 hdc into 3rd ch from hook, * sk 1 ch, work 2 hdc into next ch; rep from * across, ch 2, turn.

ROW 2: Work 1 hdc between next 2 hdc, * work 2 hdc between next 2 hdc; rep from * across, ending with 2 hdc in turning ch, ch 2, turn.

ROWS 3–34: Work 1 hdc between next 2 hdc, * work 2 hdc between next 2 hdc; rep from * across, ending with 2 hdc in turning ch, ch 2, turn.

ROW 35: Work 1 hdc between next 2 hdc, * work 2 hdc between next 2 hdc; rep from * across, ending with 2 hdc in turning ch. Fasten off.

finishing

Weave in ends. Block if desired.

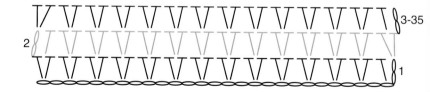

Color Commentary from Sarah London

Bold, bright dishcloths will jazz up any kitchen. I've chosen zingy orange and plum to add a burst of color. Medium to dark colors will work best in a busy, bustling kitchen.

pot holder

Multicolored pot holders add cheerfulness to any kitchen. These pot holders are suitable to make with leftover yarn from your stash; experiment with different color combinations—you really can't go wrong. Hang a collection of crocheted pot holders on the wall above your stove for an eye-catching display.

yarn

3 skeins worsted weight yarn, 1 each of 3 colors (A, B and C)

The pot holders shown here were made using Cascade 220 (100% Peruvian highland wool, 3.5oz/100g, 220yd/201m). Pot holder 1 uses colors #8339 (A), #9477 (B) and #8914 (C). Pot holder 2 uses colors #9430 (A), #7804 (B) and #8412 (C).

crochet hook

Size U.S. G/6 (4mm)

notions

Yarn needle

finished measurements

Approx. 6¾" (17cm) square (without loop)

pot holder

With color A, ch 5, join with a sl st to form a ring.

RND 1: Ch 3, work 2 dc into the ring, * ch 2, work 3 dc into the ring; rep from * twice more, ch 2, join with a sl st into top of beg ch-3. Sl st across the next 2 sts and into the corner sp.

RND 2: Ch 3, work (2 dc, ch 2, 3 dc) into corner sp, * ch 1, work (3 dc, ch 2, 3 dc) into next ch-2 corner sp; rep from * twice more, ch 1, join with a sl st into top of beg ch-3. Sl st across the next 2 sts and into the corner sp. Fasten off A.

RND 3: Join color B into any ch-2 corner sp, ch 3, work (2 dc, ch 2, 3 dc) into corner sp, * ch 1, work 3 dc into ch-1 sp, ch 1, work (3 dc, ch 2, 3 dc) into next ch-2 corner sp; rep from * twice more, ch 1, work 3 dc into ch-1 sp, ch 1, join with a sl st into top of beg ch-3. Sl st across the next 2 sts and into the corner sp.

RND 4: Ch 3, work (2 dc, ch 2, 3 dc) into corner sp, * ch 1, [work 3 dc into ch-1 sp, ch 1] twice, work (3 dc, ch 2, 3 dc) into next ch-2 corner sp; rep from * twice more, ch 1, [work 3 dc into ch-1 sp, ch 1] twice, join with a sl st into top of beg ch-3. Sl st across the next 2 sts and into the corner sp. Fasten off B.

RND 5: Join color C into any ch-2 corner sp, ch 3, work (2 dc, ch 2, 3 dc) into corner sp, * ch 1, [work 3 dc into ch-1 sp, ch 1] 3 times, work (3 dc, ch 2, 3 dc) into next ch-2 corner sp; rep from * twice more, ch 1, [work 3 dc into ch-1 sp, ch 1] 3 times, join with a sl st into top of beg ch-3. Sl st across the next 2 sts and into the corner sp.

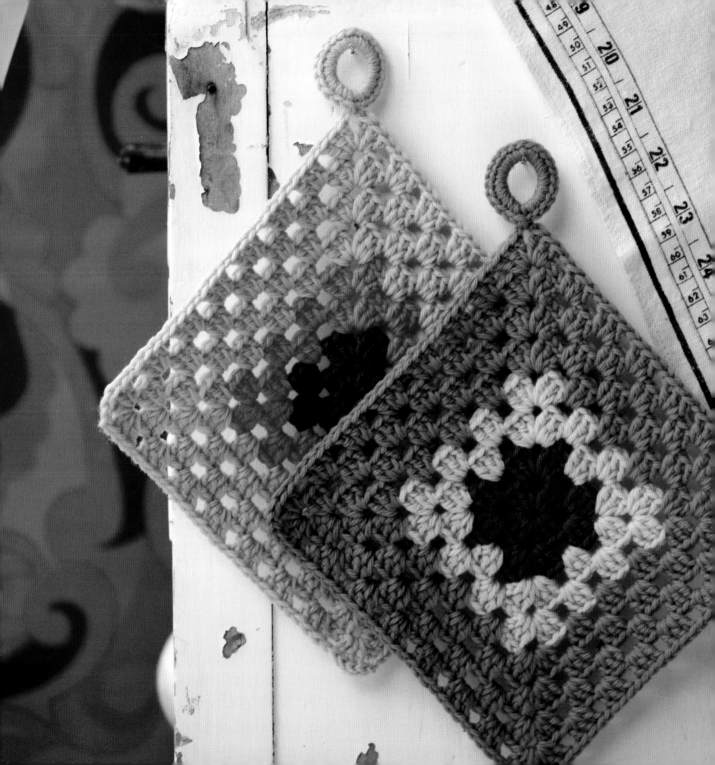

RND 6: Ch 3, work (2 dc, ch 2, 3 dc) into corner sp, * ch 1, [work 3 dc into ch-1 sp, ch 1] 4 times, work (3 dc, ch 2, 3 dc) into next ch-2 corner sp; rep from * twice more, ch 1, [work 3 dc into ch-1 sp, ch 1] 4 times, join with a sl st into top of beg ch-3. Sl st across the next 2 sts and into the corner sp.

RND 7: Ch 3, work (2 dc, ch 2, 3 dc) into corner sp, * ch 1, [work 3 dc into ch-1 sp, ch 1] 5 times, work (3 dc, ch 2, 3 dc) into next ch-2 corner sp; rep from * twice more, ch 1, [work 3 dc into ch-1 sp, ch 1] 5 times, join with a sl st into top of beg ch-3. Sl st across the next 2 sts and into the corner sp.

RND 8: Ch 3, work (2 dc, ch 2, 3 dc) into corner sp, * ch 1, [work 3 dc into ch-1 sp, ch 1] 6 times, work (3 dc, ch 2, 3 dc) into next ch-2 corner sp; rep from * twice more, ch 1, [work 3 dc into ch-1 sp, ch 1] 6 times, join with a sl st into top of beg ch-3. Sl st across the next 2 sts and into the corner sp. Fasten off.

loop

With color C, ch 12, join with a sl st to form a ring.

RND 1: Ch 1, work 22 sc into ring, join with a sl st into first sc. Fasten off, leaving a long tail for sewing.

finishing

Using tail, sew Loop in upper corner of pot holder. Weave in ends. Block if desired.

Color Commentary from Sarah London

Mixing cool and warm colors, as I have in these pot holders, often results in a interesting palette. Bring cool and warm colors from your kitchen décor together in your own set of pot holders.

Loop

grocer's tote

You will stand out from the crowd with this lively tote on your next shopping expedition. Easily transform an ordinary, sturdy jute or canvas environmentally friendly tote with vibrant bands of bold crocheted color. Both functional and attractive, this tote is perfect for running errands and transporting groceries from the store. When not in use, this tote will look equally at home hanging on the back of the kitchen door.

yarn

7 skeins worsted weight yarn, 1 each of 3 colors (A, B and C) and 4 skeins of 1 color (D)

The grocer's tote shown here was made using Cascade 220 (100% Peruvian highland wool, 3.5oz/100g, 220yd/201m) in colors #7804 (A), #9430 (B), #7830 (C) and #7828 (D).

crochet hook

U.S. size G/6 (4mm)

notions

17" × 13" × 7" (43cm × 33cm × 18cm) tote bag

Yarn needle

Sewing needle

Clear monofilament thread

finished measurements

Approx. 17" × 13" × 7" (43cm × 33cm × 18cm)

bag

With color A, ch 206.

ROW 1: Work 1 sc into 2nd ch from hook, work 1 sc into each ch across, ch 1, turn.

ROWS 2–3: Work 1 sc into each sc across, ch 1, turn.

ROW 4: Work 1 sc into each sc across, join color D, ch 3, turn.

ROW 5: Work 1 dc into first sc, * sk 2 sc, work 3 dc into next sc; rep from * across, ending with sk 2 sc, work 2 dc into last sc, ch 3, turn.

ROW 6: Work 3 dc into next sp, * sk 3 dc, work 3 dc into next sp; rep from * across, ending with 1 dc into last st, ch 3, turn.

ROW 7: Work 1 dc into first dc, * sk 3 dc, work 3 dc into next sp; rep from * across, ending with sk 3 dc, work 2 dc into last st, ch 3, turn.

Rep Rows 6–7, changing colors as follows:

ROWS 8–14: Continue with color D.

ROWS 15–16: Color B

ROWS 17–24: Color C

ROWS 25–26: Color B

ROWS 27–35: Color D

ROW 36: Work 3 dc into next sp, * sk 3 dc, work 3 dc into next sp; rep from * across, ending with 1 dc into last st, ch 1, turn. Fasten off D.

ROW 37: Join color A, work 1 sc into each st across, ch 1, turn.

ROWS 38–39: Work 1 sc into each sc across, ch 1, turn.

ROW 40: Work 1 sc into each sc across. Fasten off.

finishing

Whipstitch side edges together, matching stripes. Weave in ends. Block if desired. Place over tote, positioning seam to one side. With sewing needle and monofilament thread, whipstitch top and bottom edges to tote.

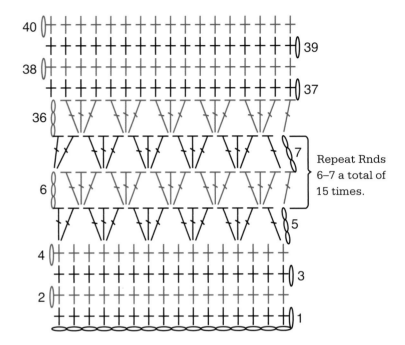

Repeat Rnds 6–7 a total of 15 times.

Reduced sample of pattern

Color Commentary from Sarah London

Bursting with bold color, the palette selected for this tote merrily blends disparate colors together. With a glaring yellow forming the foundation and a band of forest green and red, the combination is striking. Finishing with a border of pink completes the tote.

chapter four

The Dining Room

Let's add a sprinkling of crochet to the dining table with five innovative projects that you are sure to love. Be bold, be daring when next having friends over for dinner. Dress your table with a unique tablecloth bordered with granny squares in jewel tones. The colors in the Tablecloth Trim on page 72 flow from edge to edge beautifully, creating a wonderful frame for scrumptious dishes.

While the tablecloth is perfect for a special occasion, placemats are perfect for everyday use. Make a matching pair or a complete set, one for each member of the family. And no place setting is complete without a napkin holder. I'll show you how to make a granny square napkin holder in a snap! Napkin holders have never been so easy to make.

Next, a simple crocheted tea cozy made with granny squares dresses a teapot beautifully and will add color to the table. Make a tea cozy in colors to match your dinnerware (or to contrast with it!). A tea cozy is also wonderful for giving—make an extra one or two to have on hand to gift.

The last project in this chapter is perfectly suited to leave hanging all year round: a festive garland. A room with a garland is always full of happiness and cheer. Constructed of crocheted circles in various sizes, the Garland on page 90 may be made from leftover yarn. It's a fun project to use up yarn left from other projects. Your garland can be easily lengthened by adding more colorful circles to accommodate any room size.

tablecloth trim

Alter a plain tablecloth with a border of fun, funky granny squares to add sparkle to special occasions. This project is perfect for using up oddments of yarn from your stash, or you can color coordinate for a polished look. Match the edging of the granny squares to the color of your tablecloth to bring the whole project together.

yarn

Worsted weight yarn in a random assortment of colors (small amounts are okay); each square uses approx. 13yds (12m) of yarn

1 skein worsted weight yarn for edging (A)

The trim shown here was made using Cascade 220 (100% Peruvian highland wool, 3.5oz/100g, 220yd/201m). Color #8010 (A) is used for the edging.

crochet hook

U.S. G/6 (4mm)

notions

Vintage tablecloth

Yarn needle

Sewing needle

Clear monofilament thread

finished measurements

Approx. 3½" (9cm) × desired length

square

Make enough squares to cover the edges of your tablecloth.

With desired color, ch 5, join with a sl st to form a ring.

RND 1: Ch 3, work 2 dc into the ring, * ch 2, work 3 dc into the ring; rep from * twice more, ch 2, join with a sl st into top of beg ch-3. Sl st across the next 2 sts and into the corner sp.

RND 2: Ch 3, work (2 dc, ch 2, 3 dc) into corner sp, * ch 1, work (3 dc, ch 2, 3 dc) into next ch-2 corner sp; rep from * twice more, ch 1, join with a sl st into top of beg ch-3. Sl st across the next 2 sts and into the corner sp. Fasten off current color.

RND 3: Join new color into any ch-2 corner sp, ch 3, work (2 dc, ch 2, 3 dc) into corner sp, * ch 1, work 3 dc into ch-1 sp, ch 1, work (3 dc, ch 2, 3 dc) into next ch-2 corner sp; rep from * twice more, ch 1, work 3 dc into ch-1 sp, ch 1, join with a sl st into top of beg ch-3. Sl st across the next 2 sts and into the corner sp. Fasten off.

finishing

Using your preferred joining method, join squares into four strips with lengths to match your tablecloth's dimensions.

EDGING (WORK AROUND EACH STRIP)

NEXT RND: Join color A into any corner sp, ch 3, work (2 dc, ch 2, 3 dc) into corner sp, * ch 1, work 3 dc into ch-1 sp; rep from * around, working (3 dc, ch 2, 3 dc) into each corner sp, join with a sl st in top of beg ch-3. Sl st across the next 2 sts and into the corner sp. Fasten off.

Weave in ends. Block if desired. With sewing needle and monofilament thread, stitch trim in place around outer edge of tablecloth.

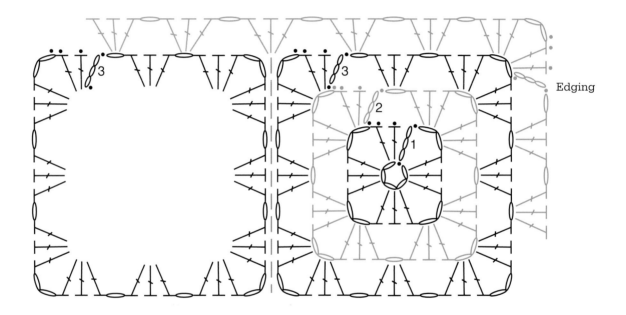

Edging

Color Commentary from Sarah London

A length of plain cotton fabric can be transformed in an instant by adding a border of assorted granny squares. Infuse your work with color—remember, more is more when creating multicolored granny squares. Use every color in your stash to create a striking cloth; balance the palette with a trimming of cream.

placemat

Placemats provide extra protection to the surface of a dining table, and they are essential at mealtimes when you have small children. These placemats are both decorative and functional and simply perfect for everyday use. Use this pattern and you'll have a lovely new set of placemats made in no time at all, one for every member of the family. A lovely scalloped edging finishes these placemats off nicely.

yarn

5 skeins worsted weight yarn, 2 skeins of 1 color (A) and 1 skein each of 3 colors (B, C and D)

The placemat shown here was made using Cascade 220 (100% Peruvian highland wool, 3.5oz/100g, 220yd/201m) in colors #8686 (A), #8010 (B), #7804 (C) and #8901 (D).

crochet hook

U.S. size G/6 (4mm)

notions

Yarn needle

finished measurements

Approx. 17" × 13½" (43cm × 34.5cm)

RND 1: With color A, ch 20, work (2 dc, ch 2, 3 dc, ch 2, 3 dc) into 4th ch from hook, * ch 1, sk 3 chs, work 3 dc into next ch **; rep from * to ** twice more, ch 1, sk 3 chs, work (3 dc, ch 2, 3 dc, ch 2, 3 dc) into next st; working in unused loops on opposite side of ch, rep from * to ** 3 times, ch 1, join with a sl st into top of beg ch-3. Sl st across the next 2 sts and into the corner sp.

RND 2: Ch 3, work (2 dc, ch 2, 3 dc) into same sp, ch 1, work (3 dc, ch 2, 3 dc) into next ch-2 corner sp, * ch 1, work 3 dc into next ch-1 sp **; rep from * to ** 3 times more, ch 1, work (3 dc, ch 2, 3 dc) into next ch-2 corner sp, ch 1, work (3 dc, ch 2, 3 dc) into next ch-2 corner sp; rep from * to ** 4 times, ch 1, join with a sl st into top of beg ch-3. Sl st across the next 2 sts and into the corner sp.

RND 3: Ch 3, work (2 dc, ch 2, 3 dc) into same sp, ch 1, work 3 dc into next ch-1 sp, ch 1, work (3 dc, ch 2, 3 dc) into next ch-2 corner sp, * ch 1, work 3 dc into next ch-1 sp **; rep from * to ** 4 times more, ch 1, work (3 dc, ch 2, 3 dc) into next ch-2 corner sp, ch 1, work 3 dc into next ch-1 sp, ch 1, work (3 dc, ch 2, 3 dc) into next ch-2 corner sp; rep from * to ** 5 times, ch 1, join with a sl st into top of beg ch-3. Sl st across the next 2 sts and into the corner sp.

RND 4: Ch 3, work (2 dc, ch 2, 3 dc) into same sp, [ch 1, work 3 dc into next ch-1 sp] twice, ch 1, work (3 dc, ch 2, 3 dc) into next ch-2 corner sp, * ch 1, work 3 dc into next ch-1 sp **; rep from * to ** 5 times more, ch 1, work (3 dc, ch 2, 3 dc) into next ch-2 corner sp, [ch 1, work 3 dc into next ch-1 sp] twice, ch 1, work (3 dc, ch 2, 3 dc) into next ch-2 corner sp; rep from * to ** 6 times, ch 1, join with a sl st into top of beg ch-3. Sl st across the next 2 sts and into the corner sp.

RND 5: Ch 3, work (2 dc, ch 2, 3 dc) into same sp, [ch 1, work 3 dc into next ch-1 sp] 3 times, ch 1, work (3 dc, ch 2, 3 dc) into next ch-2 corner sp, * ch 1, work 3 dc into next ch-1 sp **; rep from * to ** 6 times more, ch 1, work (3 dc, ch 2, 3 dc) into next ch-2 corner sp, [ch 1, work 3 dc into next ch-1 sp] 3 times, ch 1, work (3 dc, ch 2, 3 dc) into next ch-2 corner sp; rep from * to ** 7 times, ch 1, join with a sl st into top of beg ch-3. Sl st across the next 2 sts and into the corner sp.

RND 6: Ch 3, work (2 dc, ch 2, 3 dc) into same sp, [ch 1, work 3 dc into next ch-1 sp] 4 times, ch 1, work (3 dc, ch 2, 3 dc) into next ch-2 corner sp, * ch 1, work 3 dc into next ch-1 sp **; rep from * to ** 7 times more, ch 1, work (3 dc, ch 2, 3 dc) into next ch-2 corner sp, [ch 1, work 3 dc into next ch-1 sp] 4 times, ch 1, work (3 dc, ch 2, 3 dc) into next ch-2 corner sp; rep from * to ** 8 times, ch 1, join with a sl st into top of beg ch-3. Sl st across the next 2 sts and into the corner sp.

RND 7: Ch 3, work (2 dc, ch 2, 3 dc) into same sp, [ch 1, work 3 dc into next ch-1 sp] 5 times, ch 1, work (3 dc, ch 2, 3 dc) into next ch-2 corner sp, * ch 1, work 3 dc into next ch-1 sp **; rep from * to ** 8 times more, ch 1, work (3 dc, ch 2, 3 dc) into next ch-2 corner sp, [ch 1, work 3 dc into next ch-1 sp] 5 times, ch 1, work (3 dc, ch 2, 3 dc) into next ch-2 corner sp; rep from * to ** 9 times, ch 1, join with a sl st into top of beg ch-3. Sl st across the next 2 sts and into the corner sp.

RND 8: Ch 3, work (2 dc, ch 2, 3 dc) into same sp, [ch 1, work 3 dc into next ch-1 sp] 6 times, ch 1, work (3 dc, ch 2, 3 dc) into next ch-2 corner sp, * ch 1, work 3 dc into next ch-1 sp **; rep from * to ** 9 times more, ch 1, work (3 dc, ch 2, 3 dc) into next ch-2 corner sp, [ch 1, work 3 dc into next ch-1 sp] 6 times, ch 1, work (3 dc, ch 2, 3 dc) into next ch-2 corner sp; rep from * to ** 10 times, ch 1, join with a sl st into top of beg ch-3. Sl st across the next 2 sts and into the corner sp.

RND 9: Ch 3, work (2 dc, ch 2, 3 dc) into same sp, [ch 1, work 3 dc into next ch-1 sp] 7 times, ch 1, work (3 dc, ch 2, 3 dc) into next ch-2 corner sp, * ch 1, work 3 dc into next ch-1 sp **; rep from * to ** 10 times more, ch 1, work (3 dc, ch 2, 3 dc) into next ch-2 corner sp, [ch 1, work 3 dc into next ch-1 sp] 7 times, ch 1, work (3 dc, ch 2, 3 dc) into next ch-2 corner sp; rep from * to ** 11 times, ch 1, join with a sl st into top of beg ch-3. Sl st across the next 2 sts and into the corner sp.

RND 10: Ch 3, work (2 dc, ch 2, 3 dc) into same sp, [ch 1, work 3 dc into next ch-1 sp] 8 times, ch 1, work (3 dc, ch 2, 3 dc) into next ch-2 corner sp, * ch 1, work 3 dc into next ch-1 sp **; rep from * to ** 11 times more, ch 1, work (3 dc, ch 2, 3 dc) into next ch-2 corner sp, [ch 1, work 3 dc into next ch-1 sp] 8 times, ch 1, work (3 dc, ch 2, 3 dc) into next ch-2 corner sp; rep from * to ** 12 times, ch 1, join with a sl st into top of beg ch-3. Sl st across the next 2 sts and into the corner sp.

RND 11: Ch 3, work (2 dc, ch 2, 3 dc) into same sp, [ch 1, work 3 dc into next ch-1 sp] 9 times, ch 1, work (3 dc, ch 2, 3 dc) into next ch-2 corner sp, * ch 1, work 3 dc into next ch-1 sp **; rep from * to ** 12 times more, ch 1, work (3 dc, ch 2, 3 dc) into next ch-2 corner sp, [ch 1, work 3 dc into next ch-1 sp] 9 times, ch 1, work (3 dc, ch 2, 3 dc) into next ch-2 corner sp; rep from * to ** 13 times, ch 1, join with a sl st into top of beg ch-3. Sl st across the next 2 sts and into the corner sp. Fasten off A.

RND 12: Join color B into a ch-2 corner sp before a short side, ch 3, work (2 dc, ch 2, 3 dc) into corner sp, [ch 1, work 3 dc into next ch-1 sp] 10 times, ch 1, work (3 dc, ch 2, 3 dc) into next ch-2 corner sp, * ch 1, work 3 dc into next ch-1 sp **; rep from * to ** 13 times more, ch 1, work (3 dc, ch 2, 3 dc) into next ch-2 corner sp, [ch 1, work 3 dc into next ch-1 sp] 10 times, ch 1, work (3 dc, ch 2, 3 dc) into next ch-2 corner sp; rep from * to ** 14 times, ch 1, join with a sl st into top of beg ch-3. Sl st across the next 2 sts and into the corner sp.

RND 13: Ch 3, work (2 dc, ch 2, 3 dc) into corner sp, [ch 1, work 3 dc into next ch-1 sp] 11 times, ch 1, work (3 dc, ch 2, 3 dc) into next ch-2 corner sp, * ch 1, work 3 dc into next ch-1 sp **; rep from * to ** 14 times more, ch 1, work (3 dc, ch 2, 3 dc) into next ch-2 corner sp, [ch 1, work 3 dc into next ch-1 sp] 11 times, ch 1, work (3 dc, ch 2, 3 dc) into next ch-2 corner sp; rep from * to ** 15 times, ch 1, join with a sl st into top of beg ch-3. Sl st across the next 2 sts and into the corner sp. Fasten off B.

RND 14: Join color C into a ch-2 corner sp before a short side, ch 3, work (2 dc, ch 2, 3 dc) into corner sp, [ch 1, work 3 dc into next ch-1 sp] 12 times, ch 1, work (3 dc, ch 2, 3 dc) into next ch-2 corner sp, * ch 1, work 3 dc into next ch-1 sp **; rep from * to ** 15 times more, ch 1, work (3 dc, ch 2, 3 dc) into next ch-2 corner sp, [ch 1, work 3 dc into next ch-1 sp] 12 times, ch 1, work (3 dc, ch 2, 3 dc) into next ch-2 corner sp; rep from * to ** 16 times, ch 1, join with a sl st into top of beg ch-3. Sl st across the next 2 sts and into the corner sp.

RND 15: Ch 3, work (2 dc, ch 2, 3 dc) into corner sp, [ch 1, work 3 dc into next ch-1 sp] 13 times, ch 1, work (3 dc, ch 2, 3 dc) into next ch-2 corner sp, * ch 1, work 3 dc into next ch-1 sp **; rep from * to ** 16 times more, ch 1, work (3 dc, ch 2, 3 dc) into next ch-2 corner sp, [ch 1, work 3 dc into next ch-1 sp] 13 times, ch 1, work (3 dc, ch 2, 3 dc) into next ch-2 corner sp; rep from * to ** 17 times, ch 1, join with a sl st into top of beg ch-3. Sl st across the next 2 sts and into the corner sp.

RND 16: Ch 3, work (2 dc, ch 2, 3 dc) into corner sp, [ch 1, work 3 dc into next ch-1 sp] 14 times, ch 1, work (3 dc, ch 2, 3 dc) into next ch-2 corner sp, * ch 1, work 3 dc into next ch-1 sp **; rep from * to ** 17 times more, ch 1, work (3 dc, ch 2, 3 dc) into next ch-2 corner sp, [ch 1, work 3 dc into next ch-1 sp] 14 times, ch 1, work (3 dc, ch 2, 3 dc) into next ch-2 corner sp; rep from * to ** 18 times, ch 1, join with a sl st into top of beg ch-3. Sl st across the next 2 sts and into the corner sp. Fasten off.

Color Commentary from Sarah London

Chocolate, cream, pink and purple join together to form a set of practical placemats. Stick with a stable color for the center of each placemat and then have fun with the borders. Rich chocolate coordinates well with many dinner sets.

finishing

EDGING

NEXT RND: Join color D into top right ch-2 corner sp, ch 1, work (1 sc, ch 1, 3 dc, ch 1, 1 sc) into same ch-2 sp, * work (1 sc, ch 1, 2 dc, ch 1, 1 sc) into next ch-1 sp **; rep from * to ** 18 times more, work (1 sc, ch 1, 3 dc, ch 1, 1 sc) into next ch-2 corner sp; rep from * to ** 15 times, work (1 sc, ch 1, 3 dc, ch 1, 1 sc) into next ch-2 corner sp; rep from * to ** 19 times, work (1 sc, ch 1, 3 dc, ch 1, 1 sc) into next ch-2 corner sp, rep from * to ** 15 times, join with a sl st into first sc. Fasten off.

Weave in ends. Block if desired.

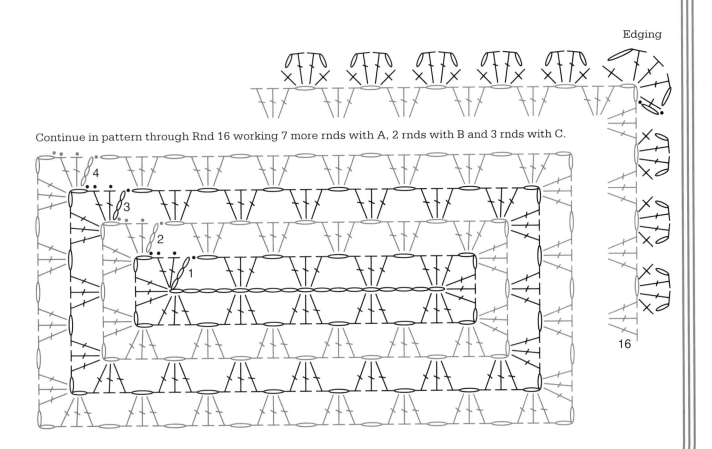

Edging

Continue in pattern through Rnd 16 working 7 more rnds with A, 2 rnds with B and 3 rnds with C.

16

napkin holder

Dress the table with these simple napkin holders the next time you have company. Napkin holders add a special touch to a table setting, not only keeping napkins neat and tidy, but also storing them decoratively at each place setting. Coordinate your napkin holders to match your tablecloth or placemats for a beautifully dressed table.

yarn

3 skeins worsted weight yarn, 1 each of 3 colors (A, B and C)

The napkin holders shown here were made using Cascade 220 (100% Peruvian highland wool, 3.5oz/100g, 220yd/201m) in colors #8010 (A), #7804 (B) and #8901 (C).

crochet hook

U.S. size G/6 (4mm)

notions

Yarn needle

finished measurements

Approx. 2¾" (7cm) square

square

Make 2 per Napkin Holder.

With color A, ch 5, join with a sl st to form a ring.

RND 1: Ch 3, work 2 dc into the ring, * ch 2, work 3 dc into the ring; rep from * twice more, ch 2, join with a sl st into top of beg ch-3. Sl st across the next 2 sts and into the corner sp. Fasten off A.

RND 2: Join color B into any ch-2 corner sp, ch 3, work (2 dc, ch 2, 3 dc) into corner sp, * ch 1, work (3 dc, ch 2, 3 dc) into next ch-2 corner sp; rep from * twice more, ch 1, join with a sl st into top of beg ch-3. Sl st across the next 2 sts and into the corner sp. Fasten off B.

RND 3: Join color C into any ch-2 corner sp, ch 3, work (2 dc, ch 2, 3 dc) into corner sp, * ch 1, work 3 dc into ch-1 sp, ch 1, work (3 dc, ch 2, 3 dc) into next ch-2 corner sp; rep from * twice more, ch 1, work 3 dc into ch-1 sp, ch 1, join with a sl st into top of beg ch-3. Sl st across the next 2 sts and into the corner sp. Fasten off C.

finishing

Place two squares tog with WS facing. Whipstitch opposite corners to form the napkin holder. Weave in ends. Block if desired.

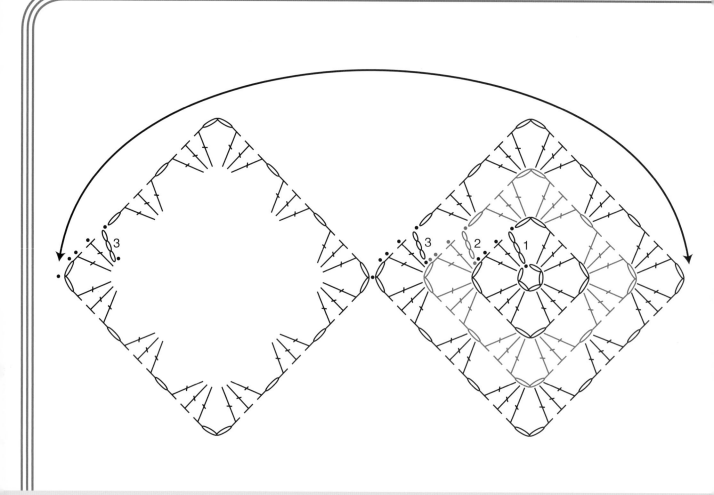

Color Commentary from Sarah London

To tie the table setting together, I selected the same colors used in the border of the Placemats on page 76 to work the Napkin Holders. Plain or patterned napkins look equally nice in these holders, or choose retro print napkins to liven each place setting.

tea cozy

I firmly believe every teapot needs a fabulous crocheted cozy. Being both functional and attractive, a tea cozy adds color to your table and keeps your tea piping hot in the pot. Work your tea cozy in pure wool for added insulation.

yarn

4 skeins worsted weight yarn, 1 each of 4 colors (A, B, C and D)

The tea cozy shown here was made using Cascade 220 (100% Peruvian highland wool, 3.5oz/100g, 220yd/201m) in colors #8415 (A), #7804 (B), #9493 (C) and #8901 (D).

crochet hook

U.S. size G/6 (4mm)

notions

Ribbon

Yarn needle

finished measurements

Approx. 7½" × 8¼" (19cm × 21cm)

square

Make 8.

With color A, ch 5, join with a sl st to form a ring.

RND 1: Ch 3, work 2 dc into the ring, * ch 2, work 3 dc into the ring; rep from * twice more, ch 2, join with a sl st into top of beg ch-3. Sl st across the next 2 sts and into the corner sp. Fasten off A.

RND 2: Join color B into any ch-2 corner sp, ch 3, work (2 dc, ch 2, 3 dc) into corner sp, * ch 1, work (3 dc, ch 2, 3 dc) into next ch-2 corner sp; rep from * twice more, ch 1, join with a sl st into top of beg ch-3. Sl st across the next 2 sts and into the corner sp. Fasten off B.

RND 3: Join color C into any ch-2 corner sp, ch 3, work (2 dc, ch 2, 3 dc) into corner sp, * ch 1, work 3 dc into ch-1 sp, ch 1, work (3 dc, ch 2, 3 dc) into next ch-2 corner sp; rep from * twice more, ch 1, work 3 dc into ch-1 sp, ch 1, join with a sl st into top of beg ch-3. Sl st across the next 2 sts and into the corner sp. Fasten off C.

RND 4: Join color D into any ch-2 corner sp, ch 3, work (2 dc, ch 2, 3 dc) into corner sp, * ch 1, [work 3 dc into ch-1 sp, ch 1] twice, work (3 dc, ch 2, 3 dc) into next ch-2 corner sp; rep from * twice more, ch 1, [work 3 dc into ch-1 sp, ch 1] twice, join with a sl st into top of beg ch-3. Sl st across the next 2 sts and into the corner sp. Fasten off D.

finishing

Join squares in 2 rows of 2 squares each using preferred method to form the Front. Repeat with second set of 4 squares to form the Back.

EDGING (WORK ON FRONT AND BACK SEPARATELY)

NEXT RND: Join color D in any ch-2 corner sp, ch 1, work 2 sc into same sp, work 1 sc into each st and ch-1 sp around, working 3 sc into each corner of panel, join with a sl st into first sc. Fasten off D.

Place Front and Back panels together with RS facing, and sl st the sides together, leaving openings for the handle and spout of your teapot. Leave the top and bottom open.

LOWER EDGE

RND 1: Join color A in any st, work 1 sc in each st around. Fasten off A.

RND 2: Join color B in any st, work 1 sc in each st around. Fasten off B.

TOP EDGE

RND 1: Join color A into any sc corresponding with a ch-1 sp below, ch 3, work 2 dc into same st, * ch 1, sk 3 sc, work 3 dc into next st; rep from * around, ch 1, sk 3 sc, join with a sl st into top of beg ch-3. Fasten off A.

RND 2: Join color D into any ch-1 sp, ch 1, work (1 sc, ch 1, 2 dc, ch 1, 1 sc) into same ch-1 sp, * work (1 sc, ch 1, 2 dc, ch 1, 1 sc) into next ch-1 sp; rep from * around, join with a sl st into first sc. Fasten off D.

Weave in ends. Block if desired. Thread ribbon through Rnd 1 of Top Edge, gather and tie in a bow.

Color Commentary from Sarah London

With a center of burgundy for depth, followed by pink and shell, then finished with purple, the granny squares that make up this Tea Cozy mirror the colors of the Placemats and Napkin Holders, completing the table setting and uniting all projects.

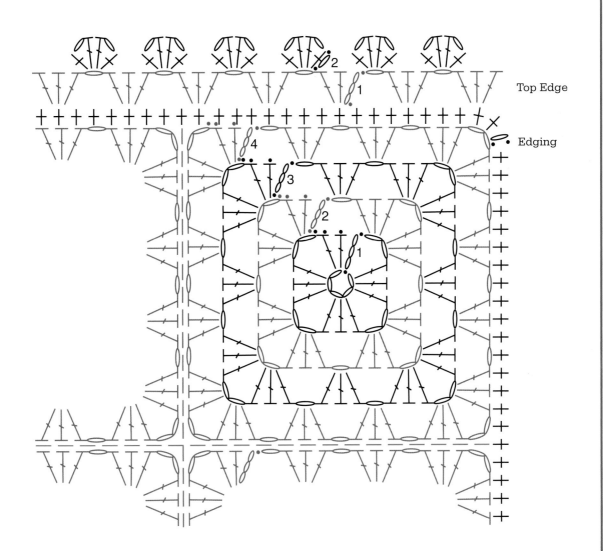

Top Edge

Edging

garland

A joyfully colored garland adds to the atmosphere at any celebration. Simple crocheted circles made in a multitude of colors shout out, "Let's celebrate!" Oddments of yarn from your stash can be used to create strands of colorful crocheted discs to hang at your next party.

yarn

8 skeins worsted weight yarn, 1 each of 8 colors (A, B, C, D, E, F, G and H)

The garland shown here was made using Cascade 220 (100% Peruvian highland wool, 3.5oz/100g, 220yd/201m) in colors #9496 (A), #9076 (B), #8509 (C), #9470 (D), #9469 (E), #7804 (F), #8905 (G) and #7826 (H).

crochet hook

U.S. size G/6 (4mm)

notions

Yarn needle

Clear monofilament thread

Sewing machine

finished measurements

118" (3m), or desired length

Work a selection of Small, Medium and Large Circles in an assortment of colors as desired.

small circle

RND 1: Ch 4, work 11 dc into 4th ch from hook, join with a sl st into top of beg ch-3. Fasten off.

medium circle

RND 1: Ch 4, work 11 dc into 4th ch from hook, join with a sl st into top of beg ch-3.

RND 2: Ch 3, work 1 dc into same st, work 2 dc into each st around, join with a sl st into top of beg ch-3. Fasten off.

large circle

RND 1: Ch 4, work 11 dc into 4th ch from hook, join with a sl st into top of beg ch-3.

RND 2: Ch 3, work 1 dc into same st, work 2 dc into each st around, join with a sl st into top of beg ch-3.

RND 3: Ch 3, work 2 dc into next st, * work 1 dc into following st, work 2 dc into next st; rep from * around, join with a sl st into top of beg ch-3. Fasten off.

finishing

Weave in ends. Block if desired. Thread your sewing machine with monofilament thread. Arrange circles as desired, and join by working a running stitch through the center of each, placing one after the other until all are joined.

Small circle

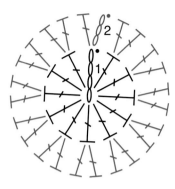

Medium circle

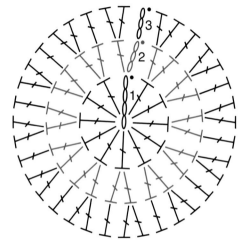

Large circle

Color Commentary from Sarah London

A string of dancing crocheted circles in an array of colors creates a pretty garland for a party. With gray scattered among the brighter colors, harmony is achieved. Garlands are meant to be boisterous; they add energy to any occasion, and more is more when it comes to colors.

chapter five

The Bedroom

Crochet a cozy nest for yourself with granny square projects, both large and small, that are perfect for the bedroom. Start with a headboard that will frame your bed. This innovative project begins with an artist's canvas; a panel of crocheted granny squares is quickly and easily secured to the canvas with amazing results. Next we will transform a bedsheet with a row of humble granny squares—you'll be surprised at the difference they will make. A fabulous textured bedsheet really does add an extra dimension to your bedding.

A bedroom would not be complete without a cozy woolen blanket to keep you warm on a cold night. A simple granny square blanket boasting a multitude of colors will be sure to keep you as warm as toast. And if for some reason the blanket doesn't keep you warm enough, try the next project: When the weather turns frightful, I turn to a hot water bottle for good, old-fashioned comfort. Adding a pretty slipcover to a hot water bottle makes it even more comforting.

You might want to make several of the last project, because who doesn't love a bed piled high with cushions! When you have so much color going on in the bedroom, you may wish to tone it down a bit. A simple crocheted cushion worked in two contrasting colors makes a statement without stealing the show. I've worked the Bold Bedroom Cushion on page 114 in classic black and white. Any pair of contrasting colors would work just fine; pluck a color from your drapes for a more coordinated look.

headboard

A granny square headboard will make a dramatic conversation piece in any bedroom. A little quirky, unusual and different, this headboard is created by covering an artist's canvas with a panel of crocheted granny squares. The crocheted panel is easily secured in place with Velcro; this makes for easy removal when it's time to update the color scheme of your bedroom.

yarn

6 skeins worsted weight yarn, 2 skeins of 1 color (A), 3 skeins of 1 color (B) and 1 skein of 1 color (C)

The headboard shown here was made using Cascade 220 (100% Peruvian highland wool, 3.5oz/100g, 220yd/201m) in colors #7808 (A), #9493 (B) and #8021 (C).

crochet hook

U.S. size H/8 (5mm)

notions

30" × 40" (76cm x 101.5cm) artist's canvas

Adhesive Velcro strips

Yarn needle

finished measurements

Approx. 30" × 40" (76cm × 101.5cm)

square

Make 20.

With color A, ch 5, join with a sl st to form a ring.

RND 1: Ch 3, work 2 dc into the ring, * ch 2, work 3 dc into the ring; rep from * twice more, ch 2, join with a sl st into top of beg ch-3. Sl st across the next 2 sts and into the corner sp.

RND 2: Ch 3, work (2 dc, ch 2, 3 dc) into corner sp, * ch 1, work (3 dc, ch 2, 3 dc) into next ch-2 corner sp; rep from * twice more, ch 1, join with a sl st into top of beg ch-3. Sl st across the next 2 sts and into the corner sp.

RND 3: Ch 3, work (2 dc, ch 2, 3 dc) into corner sp, * ch 1, work 3 dc into ch-1 sp, ch 1, work (3 dc, ch 2, 3 dc) into next ch-2 corner sp; rep from * twice more, ch 1, work 3 dc into ch-1 sp, ch 1, join with a sl st into top of beg ch-3. Sl st across the next 2 sts and into the corner sp.

RND 4: Ch 3, work (2 dc, ch 2, 3 dc) into corner sp, * ch 1, [work 3 dc into ch-1 sp, ch 1] twice, work (3 dc, ch 2, 3 dc) into next ch-2 corner sp; rep from * twice more, ch 1, [work 3 dc into ch-1 sp, ch 1] twice, join with a sl st into top of beg ch-3. Sl st across the next 2 sts and into the corner sp. Fasten off A.

RND 5: Join color B into any ch-2 corner sp, ch 3, work (2 dc, ch 2, 3 dc) into corner sp, * ch 1, [work 3 dc into ch-1 sp, ch 1] 3 times, work (3 dc, ch 2, 3 dc) into next ch-2 corner sp; rep from * twice more, ch 1, [work 3 dc into ch-1 sp, ch 1] 3 times, join with a sl st into top of beg ch-3. Sl st across the next 2 sts and into the corner sp. Fasten off B.

RND 6: Join color C into any ch-2 corner sp, ch 3, work (2 dc, ch 2, 3 dc) into corner sp, * ch 1, [work 3 dc into ch-1 sp, ch 1] 4 times, work (3 dc, ch 2, 3 dc) into next ch-2 corner sp; rep from * twice more, ch 1, [work 3 dc into ch-1 sp, ch 1] 4 times, join with a sl st into top of beg ch-3. Sl st across the next 2 sts and into the corner sp. Fasten off C.

RND 7: Join color B into any ch-2 corner sp, ch 3, work (2 dc, ch 2, 3 dc) into corner sp, * ch 1, [work 3 dc into ch-1 sp, ch 1] 5 times, work (3 dc, ch 2, 3 dc) into next ch-2 corner sp; rep from * twice more, ch 1, [work 3 dc into ch-1 sp, ch 1] 5 times, join with a sl st into top of beg ch-3. Sl st across the next 2 sts and into the corner sp. Fasten off.

finishing

Join squares in 4 rows of 5 squares each using preferred method.

BORDER

Join color B into any ch-2 corner sp and work in granny square patt as set for 3 rnds. Fasten off.

Weave in ends. Block if desired. Wrap last rnd of border around edge of canvas board and secure with Velcro.

Color Commentary from Sarah London

Regal purple mixed with apricot and biscuit create a dramatic, but not overpowering, headboard. With purple composing the center of each granny square for impact, the apricot creates the backdrop, with biscuit included for definition. Dress your bed with busy patterned vintage retro sheets for a unique look.

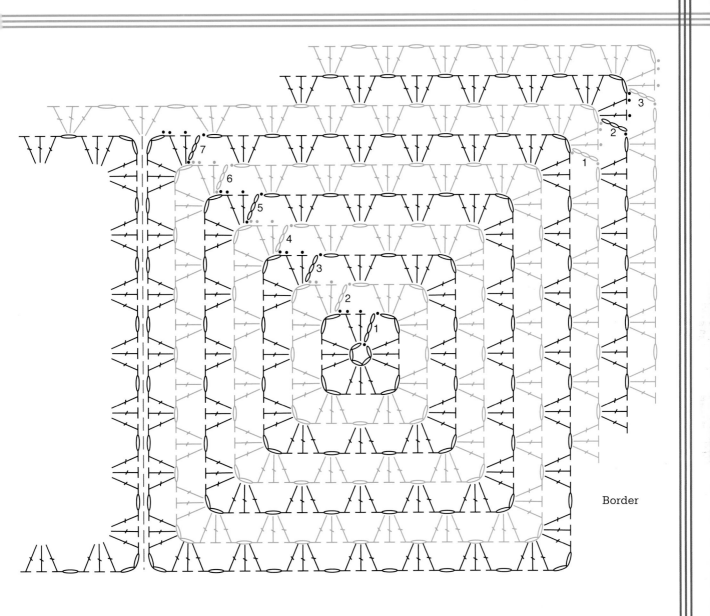

Border

bedsheet trim

Trim a flat bedsheet with a row of traditional granny squares: Your plain bedsheets will become both decorative and extra snuggly on a cold winter's evening. Vintage sheets bring color and pattern to your bed and team beautifully with crocheted granny squares. Look for psychedelic retro sheets at local thrift stores.

yarn

4 skeins worsted weight yarn, 1 each of 4 colors (A, B, C and D)

The trim shown here was made using Cascade 220 (100% Peruvian highland wool, 3.5oz/100g, 220yd/201m) in colors #8912 (A), #9477 (B), #4192 (C) and #9496 (D).

crochet hook

U.S. size G/6 (4mm)

notions

Vintage bedsheet

Yarn needle

Sewing needle

Clear monofilament thread

finished measurements

3½" × 70" (9cm × 178cm), or desired length

square

Make 20 (or number needed to fit bedsheet).

With color A, ch 5, join with a sl st to form a ring.

RND 1: Ch 3, work 2 dc into the ring, * ch 2, work 3 dc into the ring; rep from * twice more, ch 2, join with a sl st into top of beg ch-3. Sl st across the next 2 sts and into the corner sp. Fasten off A.

RND 2: Join color B into any ch-2 corner sp, ch 3, work (2 dc, ch 2, 3 dc) into corner sp, * ch 1, work (3 dc, ch 2, 3 dc) into next ch-2 corner sp; rep from * twice more, ch 1, join with a sl st into top of beg ch-3. Sl st across the next 2 sts and into the corner sp. Fasten off B.

RND 3: Join color C into any ch-2 corner sp, ch 3, work (2 dc, ch 2, 3 dc) into corner sp, * ch 1, work 3 dc into ch-1 sp, ch 1, work (3 dc, ch 2, 3 dc) into next ch-2 corner sp; rep from * twice more, ch 1, work 3 dc into ch-1 sp, ch 1, join with a sl st into top of beg ch-3. Sl st across the next 2 sts and into the corner sp. Fasten off C.

RND 4: Join color D into any ch-2 corner sp, ch 3, work (2 dc, ch 2, 3 dc) into corner sp, * ch 1, [work 3 dc into ch-1 sp, ch 1] twice, work (3 dc, ch 2, 3 dc) into next ch-2 corner sp; rep from * twice more, ch 1, [work 3 dc into ch-1 sp, ch 1] twice, join with a sl st into top of beg ch-3. Sl st across the next 2 sts and into the corner sp. Fasten off D.

finishing

Join squares in a long strip using preferred method. Weave in ends. Block if desired. With sewing needle and monofilament thread, stitch trim to top edge of sheet.

Color Commentary from Sarah London

Lemon with lilac, pink and purple adds subtle color to your bed linens. Pastel colors induce restfulness suitable for the bedroom. Trimming a plain cotton sheet with soothing pastel granny squares will update your bed linens in a flash.

bedroom blanket

Dress your bed with an extra layer of warmth in the cooler months of the year with a wonderful pure wool granny square blanket. Solid squares of crochet combine with added rounds of color to create a pretty burst of color for your bedroom. Crocheting extra squares will result in a larger blanket to fit a bed of any size.

yarn

Worsted weight yarn in a random assortment of colors, 3 colors for each square (A, B and C); each square uses approx. 222yds (203m) of yarn

2 skeins worsted weight yarn for square edging (D)

1 skein worsted weight yarn for blanket edging (E)

The blanket shown here was made using Cascade 220 (100% Peruvian highland wool, 3.5oz/100g, 220yd/201m). Color #9541 (D) is used for the square edging, and color #7830 (E) is used for the blanket edging. For a full color listing, see page 109.

crochet hook

U.S. size H/8 (5mm)

notions

Yarn needle

finished measurements

Approx. 46" × 61" (117cm × 155cm), or as desired

square

Make 12 (or number desired).

With color A, ch 5, join with a sl st to form a ring.

RND 1: Ch 3, work 2 dc into the ring, * ch 2, work 3 dc into the ring; rep from * twice more, ch 2, join with a sl st into top of beg ch-3. Sl st across the next 2 sts and into the corner sp.

RND 2: Ch 3, work (2 dc, ch 2, 3 dc) into corner sp, * ch 1, work (3 dc, ch 2, 3 dc) into next ch-2 corner sp; rep from * twice more, ch 1, join with a sl st into top of beg ch-3. Sl st across the next 2 sts and into the corner sp.

RND 3: Ch 3, work (2 dc, ch 2, 3 dc) into corner sp, * ch 1, work 3 dc into ch-1 sp, ch 1, work (3 dc, ch 2, 3 dc) into next ch-2 corner sp; rep from * twice more, ch 1, work 3 dc into ch-1 sp, ch 1, join with a sl st into top of beg ch-3. Sl st across the next 2 sts and into the corner sp.

RND 4: Ch 3, work (2 dc, ch 2, 3 dc) into corner sp, * ch 1, [work 3 dc into ch-1 sp, ch 1] twice, work (3 dc, ch 2, 3 dc) into next ch-2 corner sp; rep from * twice more, ch 1, [work 3 dc into ch-1 sp, ch 1] twice, join with a sl st into top of beg ch-3. Sl st across the next 2 sts and into the corner sp.

RND 5: Ch 3, work (2 dc, ch 2, 3 dc) into corner sp, * ch 1, [work 3 dc into ch-1 sp, ch 1] 3 times, work (3 dc, ch 2, 3 dc) into next ch-2 corner sp; rep from * twice more, ch 1, [work 3 dc into ch-1 sp, ch 1] 3 times, join with a sl st into top of beg ch-3. Sl st across the next 2 sts and into the corner sp.

RND 6: Ch 3, work (2 dc, ch 2, 3 dc) into corner sp, * ch 1, [work 3 dc into ch-1 sp, ch 1] 4 times, work (3 dc, ch 2, 3 dc) into next ch-2 corner sp; rep from * twice more, ch 1, [work 3 dc into ch-1 sp, ch 1] 4 times, join with a sl st into top of beg ch-3. Sl st across the next 2 sts and into the corner sp.

RND 7: Ch 3, work (2 dc, ch 2, 3 dc) into corner sp, * ch 1, [work 3 dc into ch-1 sp, ch 1] 5 times, work (3 dc, ch 2, 3 dc) into next ch-2 corner sp; rep from * twice more, ch 1, [work 3 dc into ch-1 sp, ch 1] 5 times, join with a sl st into top of beg ch-3. Sl st across the next 2 sts and into the corner sp.

RND 8: Ch 3, work (2 dc, ch 2, 3 dc) into corner sp, * ch 1, [work 3 dc into ch-1 sp, ch 1] 6 times, work (3 dc, ch 2, 3 dc) into next ch-2 corner sp; rep from * twice more, ch 1, [work 3 dc into ch-1 sp, ch 1] 6 times, join with a sl st into top of beg ch-3. Sl st across the next 2 sts and into the corner sp.

RND 9: Ch 3, work (2 dc, ch 2, 3 dc) into corner sp, * ch 1, [work 3 dc into ch-1 sp, ch 1] 7 times, work (3 dc, ch 2, 3 dc) into next ch-2 corner sp; rep from * twice more, ch 1, [work 3 dc into ch-1 sp, ch 1] 7 times, join with a sl st into top of beg ch-3. Sl st across the next 2 sts and into the corner sp.

RND 10: Ch 3, work (2 dc, ch 2, 3 dc) into corner sp, * ch 1, [work 3 dc into ch-1 sp, ch 1] 8 times, work (3 dc, ch 2, 3 dc) into next ch-2 corner sp; rep from * twice more, ch 1, [work 3 dc into ch-1 sp, ch 1] 8 times, join with a sl st into top of beg ch-3. Sl st across the next 2 sts and into the corner sp.

RND 11: Ch 3, work (2 dc, ch 2, 3 dc) into corner sp, * ch 1, [work 3 dc into ch-1 sp, ch 1] 9 times, work (3 dc, ch 2, 3 dc) into next ch-2 corner sp; rep from * twice more, ch 1, [work 3 dc into ch-1 sp, ch 1] 9 times, join with a sl st into top of beg ch-3. Sl st across the next 2 sts and into the corner sp. Fasten off A.

RND 12: Join color B into any ch-2 corner sp, ch 3, work (2 dc, ch 2, 3 dc) into corner sp, * ch 1, [work 3 dc into ch-1 sp, ch 1] 10 times, work (3 dc, ch 2, 3 dc) into next ch-2 corner sp; rep from * twice more, ch 1, [work 3 dc into ch-1 sp, ch 1] 10 times, join with a sl st into top of beg ch-3. Sl st across the next 2 sts and into the corner sp.

RND 13: Ch 3, work (2 dc, ch 2, 3 dc) into corner sp, * ch 1, [work 3 dc into ch-1 sp, ch 1] 11 times, work (3 dc, ch 2, 3 dc) into next ch-2 corner sp; rep from * twice more, ch 1, [work 3 dc into ch-1 sp, ch 1] 11 times, join with a sl st into top of beg ch-3. Sl st across the next 2 sts and into the corner sp.

RND 14: Ch 3, work (2 dc, ch 2, 3 dc) into corner sp, * ch 1, [work 3 dc into ch-1 sp, ch 1] 12 times, work (3 dc, ch 2, 3 dc) into next ch-2 corner sp; rep from * twice more, ch 1, [work 3 dc into ch-1 sp, ch 1] 12 times, join with a sl st into top of beg ch-3. Sl st across the next 2 sts and into the corner sp. Fasten off B.

RND 15: Join color C into any ch-2 corner sp, ch 3, work (2 dc, ch 2, 3 dc) into corner sp, * ch 1, [work 3 dc into ch-1 sp, ch 1] 13 times, work (3 dc, ch 2, 3 dc) into next ch-2 corner sp; rep from * twice more, ch 1, [work 3 dc into ch-1 sp, ch 1] 13 times, join with a sl st into top of beg ch-3. Sl st across the next 2 sts and into the corner sp. Fasten off C.

RND 16: Join color D into any ch-2 corner sp, ch 3, work (2 dc, ch 2, 3 dc) into corner sp, * ch 1, [work 3 dc into ch-1 sp, ch 1] 14 times, work (3 dc, ch 2, 3 dc) into next ch-2 corner sp; rep from * twice more, ch 1, [work 3 dc into ch-1 sp, ch 1] 14 times, join with a sl st into top of beg ch-3. Sl st across the next 2 sts and into the corner sp. Fasten off D.

finishing

Join squares in 4 rows of 3 squares each using preferred method. Join color D into any ch-2 corner sp, work in granny square patt as set for 1 rnd. Fasten off D. Join color E into any ch-2 corner sp and work 1 dc into each st and ch-1 sp around and 5 dc into each ch-2 corner sp. Fasten off E. Weave in ends. Block if desired.

Color Commentary from Sarah London

Create a vintage-styled granny square blanket by randomly placing unexpected colors together—peach, biscuit and cherry red, for example. I find that distributing murky, muddy colors among more vibrant colors in individual granny squares results in an aesthetically balanced blanket. Be mindful not to place all of your "happy" colors into one granny square; combine them with the duller colors for balance.

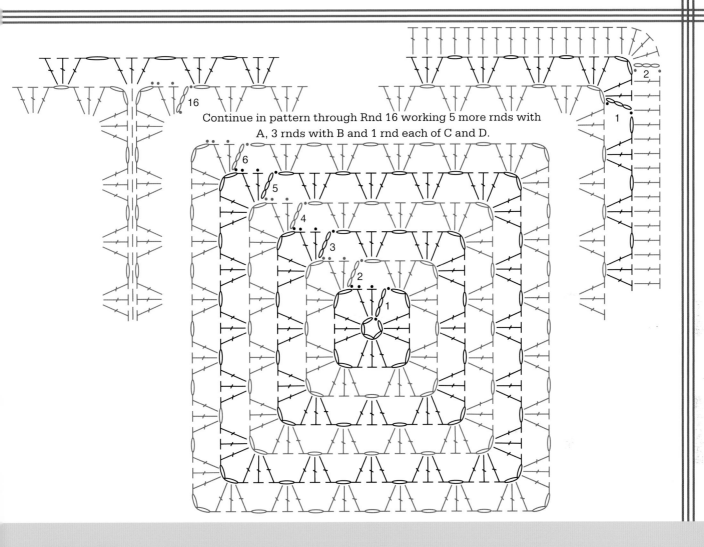

Continue in pattern through Rnd 16 working 5 more rnds with A, 3 rnds with B and 1 rnd each of C and D.

Color List

To exactly replicate the blanket I made, use the following colors:

For Square 1: #7804 (A), #9464 (B), #8914 (C)

For Square 2: #8509 (A), #7830 (B), #9421 (C)

For Square 3: #9477 (A), #9486 (B), #8901 (C)

For Square 4: #8415 (A), #8906 (B), #2415 (C)

For Square 5: #8408 (A), #8903 (B), #7803 (C)

For Square 6: #9542 (A), #8686 (B), #8905 (C)

For Square 7: #9499 (A), #8339 (B), #9473 (C)

For Square 8: #9492 (A), #8021 (B), #8895 (C)

For Square 9: #9469 (A), #9476 (B), #9076 (C)

For Square 10: #2415 (A), #8908 (B), #8894 (C)

For Square 11: #7815 (A), #9548 (B), #9493 (C)

For Square 12: #9430 (A), #4192 (B), #7812 (C)

hot water bottle cover

A crocheted cover for your hot water bottle pairs function with beauty. A simple row of practical buttons enables easy removal of the crocheted cover so that refilling your hot water bottle is a snap. Crochet your hot water bottle cover in pure wool for extra comfort, and it will provide relief from muscle aches and pains along with warmth on a chilly evening.

yarn

4 skeins worsted weight yarn, 1 each of 4 colors (A, B, C and D)

The cover shown here was made using Cascade 220 (100% Peruvian highland wool, 3.5oz/100g, 220yd/201m) in colors #7828 (A), #4192 (B), #9484 (C) and #9492 (D).

crochet hook

U.S. size G/6 (4mm)

notions

Hot water bottle

3 buttons, ½" (13mm) diameter

Yarn needle

finished measurements

Approx. 9" × 11½" (23cm × 29cm)

square

Make 12.

With color A, ch 5, join with a sl st to form a ring.

RND 1: Ch 3, work 2 dc into the ring, * ch 2, work 3 dc into the ring; rep from * twice more, ch 2, join with a sl st into top of beg ch-3. Sl st across the next 2 sts and into the corner sp. Fasten off A.

RND 2: Join color B into any ch-2 corner sp, ch 3, work (2 dc, ch 2, 3 dc) into corner sp, * ch 1, work (3 dc, ch 2, 3 dc) into next ch-2 corner sp; rep from * twice more, ch 1, join with a sl st into top of beg ch-3. Sl st across the next 2 sts and into the corner sp. Fasten off B.

RND 3: Join color C into any ch-2 corner sp, ch 3, work (2 dc, ch 2, 3 dc) into corner sp, * ch 1, work 3 dc into ch-1 sp, ch 1, work (3 dc, ch 2, 3 dc) into next ch-2 corner sp; rep from * twice more, ch 1, work 3 dc into ch-1 sp, ch 1, join with a sl st into top of beg ch-3. Sl st across the next 2 sts and into the corner sp. Fasten off C.

RND 4: Join color D into any ch-2 corner sp, ch 3, work (2 dc, ch 2, 3 dc) into corner sp, * ch 1, [work 3 dc into ch-1 sp, ch 1] twice, work (3 dc, ch 2, 3 dc) into next ch-2 corner sp; rep from * twice more, ch 1, [work 3 dc into ch-1 sp, ch 1] twice, join with a sl st into top of beg ch-3. Sl st across the next 2 sts and into the corner sp. Fasten off D.

finishing

Join squares in 3 rows of 2 squares each using preferred method to form the Front. Repeat with second set of 6 squares to form the Back.

EDGING (WORK ON FRONT AND BACK SEPARATELY)

RND 1: Join color D into any ch-2 corner sp, ch 3, work (2 dc, ch 2, 3 dc) into corner sp, * ch 1, work 3 dc into ch-1 sp; rep from * around, working (3 dc, ch 2, 3 dc) into each ch-2 corner sp, join with a sl st into top of beg ch-3. Fasten off.

With RS of Front facing, sew buttons evenly spaced along 1 edge. Align Front and Back with WS facing, and with color D, join on 3 sides (leaving button side open as well as an opening for the neck of the bottle) by working 1 sc in each ch-1 sp and dc and 3 sc in each ch-2 corner sp. On Back, opposite buttons, sc across, working ch 5 to create button loops opposite each button. Fasten off. Weave in ends. Block if desired. Insert hot water bottle. Close buttons.

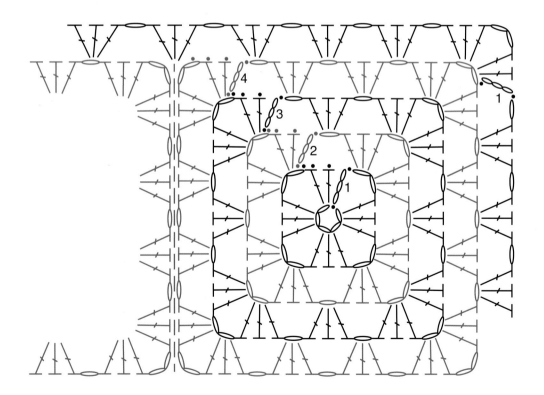

Color Commentary from Sarah London

Yolk yellow with lilac, royal blue and peach meld to create an edgy cover for your hot water bottle. The two bolder colors, yolk yellow and royal blue, are separated with a round of pale lilac to disperse their intensity. A border of peach unites the granny squares.

bold bedroom cushion

Simply stunning, this crocheted cushion is worked in two contrasting colors, resulting in a contemporary design that will lift your room without overcrowding on color. A jazzy cushion is a welcome addition to a well-dressed bed and completes the overall look of your room, adding depth and dimension to your bed.

yarn

3 skeins worsted weight yarn, 1 skein of 1 color (A) and 2 skeins of 1 color (B)

The cushion shown here was made using Cascade 220 (100% Peruvian highland wool, 3.5oz/100g, 220yd/201m) in colors #8505 (A) and #8555 (B).

crochet hook

U.S. size H/8 (5mm)

notions

14" (35.5cm) square pillow form
5 buttons, ½" (13mm) diameter
Yarn needle

finished measurements

Approx. 14" (35.5cm) square

front

With color B, ch 5, join with a sl st to form a ring.

RND 1: Ch 3, work 2 dc into the ring, * ch 2, work 3 dc into the ring; rep from * twice more, ch 2, join with a sl st into top of beg ch-3. Sl st across the next 2 sts and into the corner sp. Fasten off B.

RND 2: Join color A into any ch-2 corner sp, ch 3, work (2 dc, ch 2, 3 dc) into corner sp, * ch 1, work (3 dc, ch 2, 3 dc) into next ch-2 corner sp; rep from * twice more, ch 1, join with a sl st into top of beg ch-3. Sl st across the next 2 sts and into the corner sp. Fasten off A.

RND 3: Join color B into any ch-2 corner sp, ch 3, work (2 dc, ch 2, 3 dc) into corner sp, * ch 1, work 3 dc into ch-1 sp, ch 1, work (3 dc, ch 2, 3 dc) into next ch-2 corner sp; rep from * twice more, ch 1, work 3 dc into ch-1 sp, ch 1, join with a sl st into top of beg ch-3. Sl st across the next 2 sts and into the corner sp. Fasten off B.

RND 4: Join color A into any ch-2 corner sp, ch 3, work (2 dc, ch 2, 3 dc) into corner sp, * ch 1, [work 3 dc into ch-1 sp, ch 1] twice, work (3 dc, ch 2, 3 dc) into next ch-2 corner sp; rep from * twice more, ch 1, [work 3 dc into ch-1 sp, ch 1] twice, join with a sl st into top of beg ch-3. Sl st across the next 2 sts and into the corner sp. Fasten off A.

RND 5: Join color B into any ch-2 corner sp, ch 3, work (2 dc, ch 2, 3 dc) into corner sp, * ch 1, [work 3 dc into ch-1 sp, ch 1] 3 times, work (3 dc, ch 2, 3 dc) into next ch-2 corner sp; rep from * twice more, ch 1, [work 3 dc into ch-1 sp, ch 1] 3 times, join with a sl st into top of beg ch-3. Sl st across the next 2 sts and into the corner sp. Fasten off B.

RND 6: Join color A into any ch-2 corner sp, ch 3, work (2 dc, ch 2, 3 dc) into corner sp, * ch 1, [work 3 dc into ch-1 sp, ch 1] 4 times, work (3 dc, ch 2, 3 dc) into next ch-2 corner sp; rep from * twice more, ch 1, [work 3 dc into ch-1 sp, ch 1] 4 times, join with a sl st into top of beg ch-3. Sl st across the next 2 sts and into the corner sp. Fasten off A.

RND 7: Join color B into any ch-2 corner sp, ch 3, work (2 dc, ch 2, 3 dc) into corner sp, * ch 1, [work 3 dc into ch-1 sp, ch 1] 5 times, work (3 dc, ch 2, 3 dc) into next ch-2 corner sp; rep from * twice more, ch 1, [work 3 dc into ch-1 sp, ch 1] 5 times, join with a sl st into top of beg ch-3. Sl st across the next 2 sts and into the corner sp. Fasten off B.

RND 8: Join color A into any ch-2 corner sp, ch 3, work (2 dc, ch 2, 3 dc) into corner sp, * ch 1, [work 3 dc into ch-1 sp, ch 1] 6 times, work (3 dc, ch 2, 3 dc) into next ch-2 corner sp; rep from * twice more, ch 1, [work 3 dc into ch-1 sp, ch 1] 6 times, join with a sl st into top of beg ch-3. Sl st across the next 2 sts and into the corner sp. Fasten off A.

RND 9: Join color B into any ch-2 corner sp, ch 3, work (2 dc, ch 2, 3 dc) into corner sp, * ch 1, [work 3 dc into ch-1 sp, ch 1] 7 times, work (3 dc, ch 2, 3 dc) into next ch-2 corner sp; rep from * twice more, ch 1, [work 3 dc into ch-1 sp, ch 1] 7 times, join with a sl st into top of beg ch-3. Sl st across the next 2 sts and into the corner sp. Fasten off B.

RND 10: Join color A into any ch-2 corner sp, ch 3, work (2 dc, ch 2, 3 dc) into corner sp, * ch 1, [work 3 dc into ch-1 sp, ch 1] 8 times, work (3 dc, ch 2, 3 dc) into next ch-2 corner sp; rep from * twice more, ch 1, [work 3 dc into ch-1 sp, ch 1] 8 times, join with a sl st into top of beg ch-3. Sl st across the next 2 sts and into the corner sp. Fasten off A.

RND 11: Join color B into any ch-2 corner sp, ch 3, work (2 dc, ch 2, 3 dc) into corner sp, * ch 1, [work 3 dc into ch-1 sp, ch 1] 9 times, work (3 dc, ch 2, 3 dc) into next ch-2 corner sp; rep from * twice more, ch 1, [work 3 dc into ch-1 sp, ch 1] 9 times, join with a sl st into top of beg ch-3. Sl st across the next 2 sts and into the corner sp. Fasten off B.

RND 12: Join color A into any ch-2 corner sp, ch 3, work (2 dc, ch 2, 3 dc) into corner sp, * ch 1, [work 3 dc into ch-1 sp, ch 1] 10 times, work (3 dc, ch 2, 3 dc) into next ch-2 corner sp; rep from * twice more, ch 1, [work 3 dc into ch-1 sp, ch 1] 10 times, join with a sl st into top of beg ch-3. Sl st across the next 2 sts and into the corner sp. Fasten off A.

RND 13: Join color B into any ch-2 corner sp, ch 3, work (2 dc, ch 2, 3 dc) into corner sp, * ch 1, [work 3 dc into ch-1 sp, ch 1] 11 times, work (3 dc, ch 2, 3 dc) into next ch-2 corner sp; rep from * twice more, ch 1, [work 3 dc into ch-1 sp, ch 1] 11 times, join with a sl st into top of beg ch-3. Sl st across the next 2 sts and into the corner sp. Fasten off B.

RND 14: Join color A into any ch-2 corner sp, ch 3, work (2 dc, ch 2, 3 dc) into corner sp, * ch 1, [work 3 dc into ch-1 sp, ch 1] 12 times, work (3 dc, ch 2, 3 dc) into next ch-2 corner sp; rep from * twice more, ch 1, [work 3 dc into ch-1 sp, ch 1] 12 times, join with a sl st into top of beg ch-3. Sl st across the next 2 sts and into the corner sp. Fasten off A.

RND 15: Join color B into any ch-2 corner sp, ch 3, work (2 dc, ch 2, 3 dc) into corner sp, * ch 1, [work 3 dc into ch-1 sp, ch 1] 13 times, work (3 dc, ch 2, 3 dc) into next ch-2 corner sp; rep from * twice more, ch 1, [work 3 dc into ch-1 sp, ch 1] 13 times, join with a sl st into top of beg ch-3. Sl st across the next 2 sts and into the corner sp. Fasten off B.

back

Work as for Front, using color B throughout.

finishing

With RS of Front facing, sew buttons evenly spaced along one edge. Align Front and Back with WS facing, and with color B, join on three sides (leaving button side open) by working 1 sc in each ch-1 sp and dc and 3 sc in each ch-2 corner sp. On Back, opposite buttons, sc across, working ch 5 to create button loops opposite each button. Fasten off. Weave in ends. Block if desired. Insert pillow form. Close buttons.

Continue in pattern through Rnd 15. Working 1 rnd each with B, A, B, A, B, A and B.

Color Commentary from Sarah London

Black and white combine to create a striking modern cushion for the bedroom. Alternate rounds of each color to create a visually illuminating piece. Extracts of black are frequently introduced into homes today. I find that a small dose of black grounds the surrounding colors and adds balance to a room.

chapter six

The Bathroom and Laundry

Let's add just a hint of crochet to the bathroom and laundry, too! We will leave no room untouched. For the first project, I'll share one of my favorite home goods. I love to keep a handful of crocheted hangers in my laundry. Often, I'll reach for one when I need to hang a delicate woolen cardigan. Crochet a set of hangers in all colors of the rainbow—display them in your laundry room so you have something pretty to enjoy each time laundry day rolls around. For even more color, you can create a vibrant curtain with a length of tulle and a few crocheted granny squares to brighten your laundry room while still allowing sunshine to filter through.

Next, decorate the bathroom with a crocheted bath mat. I kept the color of my bath mat to a bare minimum, working just a few rounds of color so it wouldn't compete with my other accessories. Of course, if you'd like to make your bath mat stand out, work each round in a different color to really add some zing! To add more color to the bathroom, try adding a simple crocheted trim to a set of towels. Crocheted trim will add dimension and depth to an otherwise plain towel.

coat hangers

Crocheted coat hangers have long been a favorite of mine. They are quick and easy to work and are thoughtful, quick-to-make, inexpensive gifts. Crochet rounds of alternating double and half double crochet, and you'll have a lovely collection of colorful crocheted coat hangers made in a jiffy. A length of matching ribbon finishes each coat hanger with a pretty bow.

yarn

1 skein worsted weight yarn

The coat hangers shown here were made using Cascade 220 (100% Peruvian highland wool, 3.5oz/100g, 220yd/201m). Hanger 1 uses color #7828, Hanger 2 uses color #9492, and Hanger 3 uses color #9493.

crochet hook

U.S. size G/6 (4mm)

notions

Padded hanger

Ribbon

Yarn needle

finished measurements

Approx. 16" (40.5cm) long

RND 1: Ch 4, work 11 dc into 4th ch from hook, join with a sl st into top of beg ch-3.

RND 2: Ch 3, * work 2 dc into next st, work 1 dc into next st; rep from * 4 times more, work 2 dc into next st, join with a sl st into top of first dc.

RND 3: Ch 2, work 1 hdc into each st around, join with a sl st into top of 1st hdc.

RND 4: Ch 3, work 1 dc into each st around, join with a sl st into top of 1st dc.

Rep Rnds 3 and 4 eighteen more times.

RND 41: Ch 3, * work 2 dc tog over next 2 sts; rep from * around, join with a sl st into top of first 2 dc tog. Fasten off, leaving a long tail for finishing.

finishing

Weave in ends. Block if desired. Wrap cover around hanger. Run a gathering thread around the open end of the cover and pull to tighten. Weave in the tail to secure. Finish with a dainty bow.

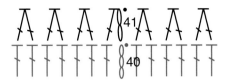

Repeat Rnds 3–4 eighteen more times.

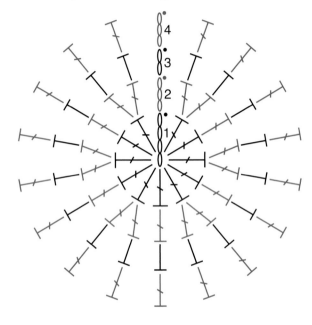

Color Commentary from Sarah London

Coat hangers look fabulous made in any color. I've chosen peachy colors and made one in a zippy yellow too. A collection of colorful crocheted coat hangers looks lovely adorning a wall or lined up in a sequence of bright colors in your wardrobe.

curtain

This fun curtain allows natural light to filter through while maintaining some privacy. Choose a lively length of colored tulle and dot it with sprightly colored granny squares to inject color and brighten a dull laundry room window. This is a room in which you can let go and play with color, beginning with the window coverings!

yarn

Worsted weight yarn in a random assortment of colors; each square uses approx. 15yds–143yds (14m–131m) of yarn

The curtain shown here was made using Cascade 220 (100% Peruvian highland wool, 3.5oz/100g, 220yd/ 201m).

crochet hook

U.S. size G/6 (4mm)

notions

Tulle curtain (of desired size)

Yarn needle

Sewing needle

Clear monofilament thread

finished measurements

Size of purchased curtain

square a

Make 3.

With desired color, ch 5, join with a sl st to form a ring.

RND 1: Ch 3, work 2 dc into the ring, * ch 2, work 3 dc into the ring; rep from * twice more, ch 2, join with a sl st into top of beg ch-3. Sl st across the next 2 sts and into the corner sp.

RND 2: Ch 3, work (2 dc, ch 2, 3 dc) into corner sp, * ch 1, work (3 dc, ch 2, 3 dc) into next ch-2 corner sp; rep from * twice more, ch 1, join with a sl st into top of beg ch-3. Sl st across the next 2 sts and into the corner sp. Fasten off current color.

RND 3: Join new color into any ch-2 corner sp, ch 3, work (2 dc, ch 2, 3 dc) into corner sp, * ch 1, work 3 dc into ch-1 sp, ch 1, work (3 dc, ch 2, 3 dc) into next ch-2 corner sp; rep from * twice more, ch 1, work 3 dc into ch-1 sp, ch 1, join with a sl st into top of beg ch-3. Sl st across the next 2 sts and into the corner sp. Fasten off current color.

RND 4: Join new color into any ch-2 corner sp, ch 3, work (2 dc, ch 2, 3 dc) into corner sp, * ch 1, [work 3 dc into ch-1 sp, ch 1] twice, work (3 dc, ch 2, 3 dc) into next ch-2 corner sp; rep from * twice more, ch 1, [work 3 dc into ch-1 sp, ch 1] twice, join with a sl st into top of beg ch-3. Sl st across the next 2 sts and into the corner sp. Fasten off current color.

RND 5: Join new color into any ch-2 corner sp, ch 3, work (2 dc, ch 2, 3 dc) into corner sp, * ch 1, [work 3 dc into ch-1 sp, ch 1] 3 times, work (3 dc, ch 2, 3 dc) into next ch-2 corner sp; rep from * twice more, ch 1, [work 3 dc into ch-1 sp, ch 1] 3 times, join with a sl st into top of beg ch-3. Sl st across the next 2 sts and into the corner sp. Fasten off current color.

square b

Make 11.

Work as for Rnds 1–3 of Square A, changing colors every rnd.

square c

Make 1.

Work as for Rnds 1–4 of Square A, changing colors every rnd.

square d

Make 1.

Work as for Rnds 1–4 of Square A, changing colors for Rnds 3–4.

finishing

Weave in ends. Block if desired. Arrange as desired on curtain. With sewing needle and monofilament thread, stitch in place.

Squares C & D

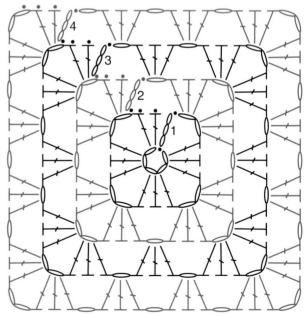

Square A

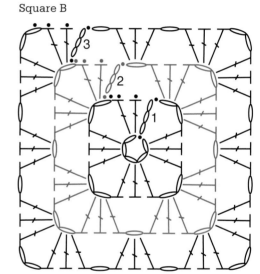

Square B

Color Commentary from Sarah London

A selection of orphan granny squares in a variety of sizes and colors will quickly turn your laundry room from gloomy to gorgeous. You can go overboard with color in this project because the majority of appliances and structures in the laundry room are white, so there's no worry about clashing.

bath mat

Both pretty and functional, this bath mat is worked with just a hint of color. Choose colors to match the other accessories in your bathroom, or use random leftover colors to make a more playful version. It's beautifully absorbent when made from pure wool and gentle on bare feet! A decorative scalloped edge finishes this bath mat nicely.

yarn

5 skeins worsted weight yarn, 1 each of 5 colors (A, B, C, D and E)

The mat shown here was made using Cascade 220 (100% Peruvian highland wool, 3.5oz/100g, 220yd/201m) in colors #8505 (A), #7830 (B), #9076 (C), #4192 (D) and #8908 (E).

crochet hook

Size U.S. G/6 (4mm)

notions

Yarn needle

finished measurements

21" × 17" (53.5cm × 43cm)

RND 1: With color A, ch 20, work (2 dc, ch 2, 3 dc, ch 2, 3 dc) into 4th ch from hook, * ch 1, sk 3 sts, work 3 dc into next st **; rep from * to ** twice more, ch 1, sk 3 sts, work (3 dc, ch 2, 3 dc, ch 2, 3 dc) into next st; working in unused loops on opposite side of ch, rep from * to ** 3 times, ch 1, join with a sl st into top of beg ch-3. Sl st across the next 2 sts and into the corner sp.

RND 2: Ch 3, work (2 dc, ch 2, 3 dc) into same sp, ch 1, work (3 dc, ch 2, 3 dc) into next ch-2 corner sp, * ch 1, work 3 dc into next ch-1 sp **; rep from * to ** 3 times more, ch 1, work (3 dc, ch 2, 3 dc) into next ch-2 corner sp, ch 1, work (3 dc, ch 2, 3 dc) into next ch-2 corner sp; rep from * to ** 4 times, ch 1, join with a sl st into top of beg ch-3. Sl st across the next 2 sts and into the corner sp.

RND 3: Ch 3, work (2 dc, ch 2, 3 dc) into same sp, ch 1, work 3 dc into next ch-1 sp, ch 1, work (3 dc, ch 2, 3 dc) into next ch-2 corner sp, * ch 1, work 3 dc into next ch-1 sp **; rep from * to ** 4 times more, ch 1, work (3 dc, ch 2, 3 dc) into next ch-2 corner sp, ch 1, work 3 dc into next ch-1 sp, ch 1, work (3 dc, ch 2, 3 dc) into next ch-2 corner sp; rep from * to ** 5 times, ch 1, join with a sl st into top of beg ch-3. Sl st across the next 2 sts and into the corner sp.

RND 4: Ch 3, work (2 dc, ch 2, 3 dc) into same sp, [ch 1, work 3 dc into next ch-1 sp] twice, ch 1, work (3 dc, ch 2, 3 dc) into next ch-2 corner sp, * ch 1, work 3 dc into next ch-1 sp **; rep from * to ** 5 times more, ch 1, work (3 dc, ch 2, 3 dc) into next ch-2 corner sp, [ch 1, work 3 dc into next ch-1 sp] twice, ch 1, work (3 dc, ch 2, 3 dc) into next ch-2 corner sp; rep from * to ** 6 times, ch 1, join with a sl st into top of beg ch-3. Sl st across the next 2 sts and into the corner sp.

RND 5: Ch 3, work (2 dc, ch 2, 3 dc) into same sp, [ch 1, work 3 dc into next ch-1 sp] 3 times, ch 1, work (3 dc, ch 2, 3 dc) into next ch-2 corner sp, * ch 1, work 3 dc into next ch-1 sp **; rep from * to ** 6 times more, ch 1, work (3 dc, ch 2, 3 dc) into next ch-2 corner sp, [ch 1, work 3 dc into next ch-1 sp] 3 times, ch 1, work (3 dc, ch 2, 3 dc) into next ch-2 corner sp; rep from * to ** 7 times, ch 1, join with a sl st into top of beg ch-3. Sl st across the next 2 sts and into the corner sp.

RND 6: Ch 3, work (2 dc, ch 2, 3 dc) into same sp, [ch 1, work 3 dc into next ch-1 sp] 4 times, ch 1, work (3 dc, ch 2, 3 dc) into next ch-2 corner sp, * ch 1, work 3 dc into next ch-1 sp **; rep from * to ** 7 times more, ch 1, work (3 dc, ch 2, 3 dc) into next ch-2 corner sp, [ch 1, work 3 dc into next ch-1 sp] 4 times, ch 1, work (3 dc, ch 2, 3 dc) into next ch-2 corner sp; rep from * to ** 8 times, ch 1, join with a sl st into top of beg ch-3. Sl st across the next 2 sts and into the corner sp.

RND 7: Ch 3, work (2 dc, ch 2, 3 dc) into same sp, [ch 1, work 3 dc into next ch-1 sp] 5 times, ch 1, work (3 dc, ch 2, 3 dc) into next ch-2 corner sp, * ch 1, work 3 dc into next ch-1 sp **; rep from * to ** 8 times more, ch 1, work (3 dc, ch 2, 3 dc) into next ch-2 corner sp, [ch 1, work 3 dc into next ch-1 sp] 5 times, ch 1, work (3 dc, ch 2, 3 dc) into next ch-2 corner sp; rep from * to ** 9 times, ch 1, join with a sl st into top of beg ch-3.

Color Commentary from Sarah London

With a crisp, clean white for the center of the bath mat, red is introduced to add structure and outline the design. A hint of pale aqua follows to create contrast. Fresh white is then worked to separate the next color sequence of lilac and aqua.

For the remainder of the mat, work in patt as set, changing colors as follows:

RNDS 8–11: Color A

RNDS 12–13: Color B

RNDS 14–15: Color C

RNDS 16–17: Color A

RNDS 18–19: Color D

RNDS 20–21: Color E

finishing

EDGING

NEXT RND: Join color A into top right ch-2 corner sp, ch 1, work (1 sc, ch 1, 3 dc, ch 1, 1 sc) into same ch-2 sp, * work (1 sc, ch 1, 2 dc, ch 1, 1 sc) into next ch-1 sp **; rep from * to ** 23 times more, work (1 sc, ch 1, 3 dc, ch 1, 1 sc) into next ch-2 corner sp; rep from * to ** 20 times, work (1 sc, ch 1, 3 dc, ch 1, 1 sc) into next ch-2 corner sp; rep from * to ** 24 times, work (1 sc, ch 1, 3 dc, ch 1, 1 sc) into next ch-2 corner sp; rep from * to ** 20 times, join with a sl st into first sc. Fasten off.

Weave in ends. Block if desired.

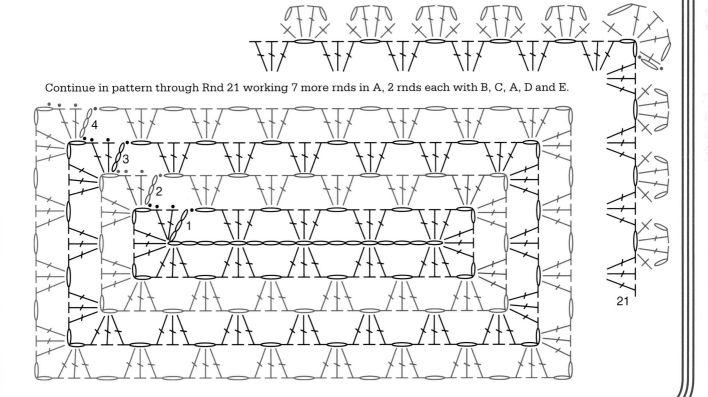

Edging

Continue in pattern through Rnd 21 working 7 more rnds in A, 2 rnds each with B, C, A, D and E.

21

towel trim

A matching towel set looks inviting in a guest bathroom or is perfect for everyday use in the main bathroom of your home. Decorate a set of plain bathroom towels by adding texture and dimension with an attractive crocheted border. Coordinate colors to match the paint color, accessories or art in your bathroom.

yarn

4 skeins worsted weight yarn, 1 each of 4 colors (A, B, C and D)

The trim shown here was made using Cascade 220 (100% Peruvian highland wool, 3.5oz/100g, 220yd/201m) in colors #7830 (A), #9493 (B), #9469 (C) and #4192 (D).

crochet hook

U.S. size G/6 (4mm)

notions

Standard size bath towel

Yarn needle

Sewing needle

Clear monofilament thread

finished measurements

27" (68.5cm) wide

RND 1: With color A, ch 112, work (2 dc, ch 2, 3 dc, ch 2, 3 dc) in 4th ch from hook, * ch 1, sk 3 sts, work 3 dc into next st **; rep from * to ** 25 times more, ch 1, sk 3 sts, work (3 dc, ch 2, 3 dc, ch 2, 3 dc) into next st; working in unused loops on opposite side of ch rep from * to ** 26 times, ch 1, join with a sl st in top of beg ch-3. Sl st across the next 2 sts and into the corner sp. Fasten off A.

RND 2: Join color B into last ch-2 corner sp, ch 3, work (2 dc, ch 2, 3 dc) into same sp, ch 1, work (3 dc, ch 2, 3 dc) into next ch-2 corner sp, * ch 1, work 3 dc into next ch-1 sp **; rep from * to ** 26 times more, work (3 dc, ch 2, 3 dc) into next ch-2 corner sp, ch 1, work (3 dc, ch 2, 3 dc) into next ch-2 corner sp; rep from * to ** 27 times, ch 1, join with a sl st into top of beg ch-3. Sl st across the next 2 sts and into the corner sp. Fasten off B.

RND 3: Join color C into last ch-2 corner sp, ch 3, work (2 dc, ch 2, 3 dc) into same sp, ch 1, work 3 dc into next ch-1 sp, ch 1, work (3 dc, ch 2, 3 dc) into next ch-2 corner sp, * ch 1, work 3 dc into next ch-1 sp **; rep from * to ** 27 times more, work (3 dc, ch 2, 3 dc) into next ch-2 corner sp, ch 1, work 3 dc into next ch-1 sp, ch 1, work (3 dc, ch 2, 3 dc) into next ch-2 corner sp; rep from * to ** 28 times, ch 1, join with a sl st into top of beg ch-3. Sl st across the next 2 sts and into the corner sp. Fasten off C.

RND 4: Join color D into last ch-2 corner sp, ch 3, work (2 dc, ch 2, 3 dc) into same sp, ch 1, [work 3 dc into next ch-1 sp, ch 1] twice, work (3 dc, ch 2, 3 dc) into next ch-2 corner sp, * ch 1, work 3 dc into next ch-1 sp **; rep from * to ** 28 times more, work (3 dc, ch 2, 3 dc) into next ch-2 corner sp, ch 1, [work 3 dc into next ch-1 sp, ch 1] twice, work (3 dc, ch 2, 3 dc) into next ch-2 corner sp; rep from * to ** 29 times, ch 1, join with a sl st into top of beg ch-3. Sl st across the next 2 sts and into the corner sp. Fasten off D.

RND 5: Join color A into last ch-2 corner sp, ch 3, work (2 dc, ch 2, 3 dc) into same sp, ch 1, [work 3 dc into next ch-1 sp, ch 1] 3 times, work (3 dc, ch 2, 3 dc) into next ch-2 corner sp, * ch 1, work 3 dc into next ch-1 sp **; rep from * to ** 29 times more, work (3 dc, ch 2, 3 dc) into next ch-2 corner sp, ch 1, [work 3 dc into next ch-1 sp, ch 1] 3 times, work (3 dc, ch 2, 3 dc) into next ch-2 corner sp; rep from * to ** 30 times, ch 1, join with a sl st into top of beg ch-3. Sl st across the next 2 sts and into the corner sp. Fasten off A.

finishing

Weave in ends. Block if desired. With sewing needle and monofilament thread, stitch in place along edge of towel.

Reduced sample of pattern

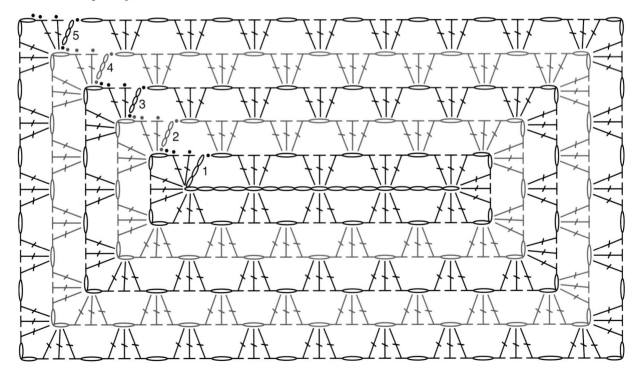

Color Commentary from Sarah London

I coordinated the palette of this towel trim with the bath mat and attached it to pure white towels. Pair your bordered towels with solid-colored bath towels and extract a single color from the palette for a coordinated look.

general crochet information

stitch terminology and symbols

In the instructions for the projects, I have favored U.S. crochet terms. Refer to this box for the U.K. or Australian equivalent.

US CROCHET TERM		UK OR AU CROCHET TERM
chain (ch)	⬭	chain (ch)
slip stitch (sl st)	•	slip stitch (ss)
single crochet (sc)	†	double crochet (dc)
half double crochet (hdc)	⊤	half treble (htr)
double crochet (dc)	⊤	treble (tr)

substituting yarns

All of the projects in this book were made using Cascade 220. Visit the Cascade Yarns website to find a retailer near you: www.cascadeyarns.com. If you decide to use a yarn other than Cascade 220, be sure to select a yarn of the same weight. Even after checking that the recommended gauge on the yarn you plan to substitute is the same as for the yarn listed in the pattern, make sure to crochet a swatch to ensure that the yarn and hook you are using will produce a fabric you are happy with.

crochet hook conversions

U.S. SIZE	DIAMETER (MM)
B/1	2.25
C/2	2.75
D/3	3.25
E/4	3.5
F/5	3.75
G/6	4
7	4.5
H/8	5
I/9	5.5
J/10	6
K/10½	6.5
L/11	8
M/13, N/13	9
N/15, P/15	10
P/Q	15
Q	16
S	19

yarn weight guidelines

Because the names given to different weights of yarn can vary widely depending on the country of origin or the yarn manufacturer's preference, the Craft Yarn Council of America has put together a standard yarn weight system to impose a bit of order on the sometimes unruly yarn labels. Look for a picture of a skein of yarn with a number 0–6 on most kinds of yarn to figure out its "official" weight. The information in the chart below is taken from www.yarnstandards.com.

	LACE (0) **0 LACE**	SUPER FINE (1) **1 SUPER FINE**	FINE (2) **2 FINE**	LIGHT (3) **3 LIGHT**	MEDIUM (4) **4 MEDIUM**	BULKY (5) **5 BULKY**	SUPER BULKY (6) **6 SUPER BULKY**
Weight	fingering, 10-count crochet thread	sock, fingering, 2ply, 3ply	sport, baby, 4ply	light worsted, DK	worsted, afghan, aran	chunky, craft, rug	super-chunky, bulky, roving
Crochet Gauge Range*	32–42 sts	21–32 sts	16–20 sts	12–17 sts	11–14 sts	8–11 sts	5–9 sts
Recommended Hook Range**	Steel*** 6, 7, 8 Regular hook B/1 (1.4mm–2.25mm)	B/1 to E/4 (2.25mm–3.5mm)	E/4 to 7 (3.5mm–4.5mm)	7 to I/9 (4.5mm–5.5mm)	I/9 to K/10½ (5.5mm–6.5mm)	K/10½ to M/13 (6.5mm–9mm)	M/13 and larger (9mm and larger)

Notes:
* Gauge (what U.K. crocheters call "tension") is measured over 4" (10cm) in single crochet (except for Lace [0], which is worked in double crochet).
** U.S. hook sizes are given first, with U.K. equivalents in parentheses.
*** Steel crochet hooks are sized differently from regular hooks—the higher the number, the smaller the hook, which is the reverse of regular hook sizing.

index

acknowledgments

Eternally grateful to:

- ❤ My children—Emma, Jack and Thomas—who perhaps held the gray card more times than they would have liked.

- ❤ My husband, Matthew, who has endured skeins of yarn in virtually every room of the house for the last twenty-one years.

- ❤ My father, John, for his expertise in cameras and contracts.

- ❤ My mother, Robyn, who believed.

- ❤ My grandmother Dallys, who ignited the passion.

- ❤ My friend Donna, for her encouragement.

- ❤ My editor, Jennifer, who moved heaven and earth to have this book published.

- ❤ The photography department at F+W Media, Inc., who worked with each photo I submitted, with or without the gray card.

- ❤ Cascade Yarns, for providing a superb palette of delectable yarns.

about the author

Sarah has been immersed in crochet for most of her life. Her grandmother taught her to crochet at an early age. She started with granny squares and quickly progressed to making crocheted roses.

With a love of color, Sarah works traditional motifs in bursts of bold color and modernizes crochet for the twenty-first century.

She publishes a monthly crochet e-zine, *Hip to Hook*, which is distributed worldwide.

She actively supports various charitable organizations across the globe and founded Crochet-a-Rainbow in January 2011.

Sarah lives on the east coast of Australia with her husband and three children.

www.fwmedia.com

15 14 13 12 11   5 4 3 2 1

DISTRIBUTED IN CANADA BY FRASER DIRECT
100 Armstrong Avenue
Georgetown, ON, Canada L7G 5S4
Tel: (905) 877-4411

DISTRIBUTED IN THE U.K. AND EUROPE BY F&W MEDIA INTERNATIONAL
Brunel House, Newton Abbot, Devon, TQ12 4PU, England
Tel: (+44) 1626 323200, Fax: (+44) 1626 323319
Email: enquiries@fwmedia.com

DISTRIBUTED IN AUSTRALIA BY CAPRICORN LINK
P.O. Box 704, S. Windsor NSW, 2756 Australia
Tel: (02) 4577-3555

SRN: W0657
ISBN-13: 978-1-4403-1294-6

Edited by Jennifer Claydon
Cover designed by Michelle Thompson and Geoff Raker
Designed by Michelle Thompson and Geoff Raker
Production coordinated by Greg Nock
Photography by Sarah London

To my children,

Emma, Jack and Thomas

I love you . . . you are my sunshine.

Metric Conversion Chart

Measurements have been given in Imperial inches with metric conversions following—use one or the other as they are not interchangeable. The most accurate results will be obtained using inches.

To convert	to	multiply by
Inches	Centimeters	2.54
Centimeters	Inches	0.4
Feet	Centimeters	30.5
Centimeters	Feet	0.03
Yards	Meters	0.9
Meters	Yards	1.1

Find a free bonus project online!

Visit **store.marthapullen.com/Granny_Square_Love_Pattern** to get your free copy of the pattern for this pillowcase edging.

  fw media

 Become a fan on Facebook at fwcraft

Follow us on Twitter at fwcraft